WALKING WITH

WALKING WITH LIONS

Tales from a Diplomatic Past

K. NATWAR SINGH

HarperCollins *Publishers* India

First published in India in 2013 by
HarperCollins *Publishers* India

Copyright © K. Natwar Singh 2013

P-ISBN: 978-93-5029-346-1
E-ISBN: 978-93-5029-899-2

4 6 8 10 9 7 5 3

K. Natwar Singh asserts the moral right
to be identified as the author of this work.

All rights reserved. No part of this publication may be reproduced, stored in a retrieval system, or transmitted, in any form or by any means, electronic, mechanical, photocopying, recording or otherwise, without the prior permission of the publishers.

HarperCollins *Publishers*
A-75, Sector 57, Noida 201301, India
77-85 Fulham Palace Road, London W6 8JB, United Kingdom
Hazelton Lanes, 55 Avenue Road, Suite 2900, Toronto, Ontario M5R 3L2
and 1995 Markham Road, Scarborough, Ontario M1B 5M8, Canada
25 Ryde Road, Pymble, Sydney, NSW 2073, Australia
10 East 53rd Street, New York NY 10022, USA

Typeset in 15/16 Adobe Thai by
Jojy Philip, New Delhi 110 015

Printed and bound at
Thomson Press (India) Ltd

For my son Jagat
and grandchildren Hanut and Himmat

Contents

A Prefatory Note

During my long life I have met and got to know a large number of people of character, calibre, courage, sensitivity, vision and unquestionable distinction. This has been a blessing. The carnival of personalities includes politicians, authors, artists, painters, bureaucrats and sportsmen from many parts of the globe. Inevitably, they have enriched my life, broadened my vision and refined my sensibilities. Several inspired me in no small measure. I learnt to face adversity with confidence and detachment, if not serenity. Wisdom may have eluded me, but not the joy of living and giving.

These fifty articles appeared in *Mail Today* in 2011–12. I enjoyed writing them and was pleased by the interest they aroused. No -ism infects them. No preaching disfigures them.

This volume is the brainchild of Aroon Purie, editor-in-chief of the India Today Group. I thank him in all sincerity. To Krishan Chopra, Publisher and Chief Editor, HarperCollins *Publishers* India, I express my gratitude. For the title I suggested 'The Pleasures and Perils of Diplomacy'—he avoided commenting on my inanity and came up with a gem. Also thanks to Debasri Rakshit for being a tolerant editor.

K. Natwar Singh

1

An Ill-tempered PM

On 23 March 1977, Morarji bhai Desai was sworn in as prime minister. The next day a top-secret telegram from the Ministry of External Affairs was placed on my office table. It said that I should immediately take leave. No explanation was given. I was flabbergasted. Later I discovered that my being 'Indira Gandhi's man in London' had done me in.

Morarji Desai arrived in London in early June to attend the Commonwealth Prime Ministers' Conference. To my great surprise his host was High Commissioner B.K. Nehru. After all, he had, like me, defended the Emergency. Later I learnt that the good Nehru had got in touch with the new PM, whom he knew well, and had invited him to stay with him at 9, Kensington Palace Gardens, the ducal residence of the high commissioner. (Mrs Gandhi was livid when she heard that her second cousin was playing host to her principal political opponent.)

I became a non-person overnight as far as the high commissioner was concerned. My wife was recovering from a gall bladder operation. Our two children aged seven and six had not fully recovered from their tonsil operations. My mother-in-law kept in touch with us. She had been fed on horror tales about her son-in-law's crimes during the Emergency. After differences with Indira Gandhi, she had gone over to Morarji Desai's faction a couple of years back. She was now one of the general secretaries of the Janata Party, and was in an unenviable predicament. Personal and political loyalties collided. My paramount worry was regarding my next posting. How long was I to keep cooling my heels? No one in the Ministry of External Affairs and hardly anyone in the high commission was in the least interested. Only two IFS officers did not desert me. One of them retired a few years ago. He too suffered on my account. When I became foreign minister, I made sure he got his due.

I have strong nerves. Defiance comes to me with ease. I did not and do not suffer fools. I also knew my worth. My five years with Indira Gandhi had bestowed on me a distinction few bureaucrats attain. My service record was the envy of many.

On the third day after Morarji Desai's arrival, B.K. Nehru rang me up. What he said appalled me. 'Natwar, the PM tells me that you held a champagne party on 26 June 1975 [the day the Emergency was declared] at India House. Did you?' I replied, 'Bijju bhai, on that unforgettable day you and I were at India House the whole time answering questions from the media. Besides, the news of the never-held party could not have remained a secret from the media, British and Indian, because the phantom guests would have certainly spread the news.' To pull his leg I added, 'Are you sure *you* did not give a champagne party at *your* residence?' He had a sense of humour. Laughing, he put the phone down.

Two days later the HC said the PM wished to see the 'discretionary grant' register. 'How much did you spend out of it?' Again I was outraged. I informed the HC that we had asked for a grant of £5,000, out of which we had spent only £450. I immediately had the grant register sent to him as the PM wished to see it. He obviously had nothing better to do. He did not believe what he saw. 'This is a false record. I know Indira used to send cash to Natwar Singh by diplomatic bags!'

We all knew Desai had not the foggiest idea how diplomatic bags are handled. On arrival the officer, a first secretary, has the bag opened in the presence of several assistants, and the contents are distributed to the concerned persons—letters, files, Indian newspapers. Then a list is drawn up. All these facts were placed before the prime minister, who dismissed them immediately. He apparently even commented to the HC that 'Indira must have sent the cash by some other means'.

I was naturally anxious to know of my next posting. I was relieved to be informed that I had been appointed high commissioner to Zambia. I had been twice to the country with the decolonization committee. More importantly, I knew President Kenneth Kaunda well. He had come to New York in 1962 to appear before the committee as a petitioner, to expose the inequities of British rule in Northern Rhodesia, as it then was. Our instructions were to support him. I invited him for lunch and gave him a lift in my car. The permanent representative, C.S. Jha, an able diplomat, did not have any time to spare for Kaunda.

Two years later he came to the US as the prime minister of Zambia. From Washington he travelled to New York by train. The permanent representatives of the African and Commonwealth countries were at the station to receive him. When he spotted Jha he asked, 'Where is Mr Natwar Singh?'

Had Desai and the MEA known this I would never have been sent to Zambia. Lusaka is 4,000 feet above sea level. The climate could not be better and there were no stacks of files to deal with. I spent two-and-a-half pleasant and rewarding years in Zambia.

I had easy access to the president. I played a lot of tennis, wrote a book on Suraj Mal, the real founder of Bharatpur, my home state. It was published in London. Lusaka was not London. But it had many things to its favour.

A few days before leaving London, a colleague of mine handed me an invaluable document, 'Dietary Preferences of the Prime Minister'. Here it goes:

> Carrot juice: only from the deep pink carrot grown in northern India.
> Lunch: 5 pieces of garlic, must be freshly peeled before serving. Cow's milk (lukewarm). Honey. Fresh paneer slices.
> Fruit: banana, papaya, apple, pear, leechi, cherries, apricots and alphonso mangoes.
> Dry fruit: cashew nuts, *badaam*, pista, *moongphali dana* (roasted).

Indian sweets: *sandesh*, *pera*, *humchum*, *rasmalai*, *rasgoolla*, *gajar ka halwa*.

The dinner menu was even more appetizing. His favourite drink was not mentioned. Everyone knew what it was.

Some Gandhian diet for a pseudo-Gandhian.

2

A Spat with Morarji Desai

For all writers of history Morarji bhai Desai is a huge disappointment. When he died in 1995, at the age of ninety-nine, no comets were seen. The heavens did not blaze forth his death. His personality was that of a one-dimensional man. He was a competent servant of state but not a tribune of the people.

I was not an admirer. I actually had the chutzpah to take him on, thus earning his wrath when he was prime minister. I was cussedly defiant. In retrospect, I do concede that I should have been more circumspect. Here is the story. In August 1977 I arrived in Lusaka, capital of Zambia, to take up my post as high commissioner. The politics of southern Africa were in turmoil, and Zambia was a frontline state. Several important leaders of the freedom movements in South Africa, South-West Africa (now Namibia) and Southern Rhodesia (now Zimbabwe) found refuge in Zambia. These included Oliver Tambo of the African National Congress; Nelson Mandela was in prison and Tambo had been carrying the torch of the South African freedom movement. From

Southern Rhodesia there was the well-known Joshua Nkomo, who had spent many years in prison (Robert Mugabe was in exile in Mozambique). From South-West Africa there was Sam Nujoma, who would later become the founding president of Namibia. India was helping each of them in every way except supplying arms. I was personally in touch with these leaders.

Prime Minister Morarji Desai's knowledge of and interest in Africa was abysmal. This had not been the case with Jawaharlal Nehru, Indira Gandhi and Rajiv Gandhi. The president of Zambia, Kenneth Kaunda, was an African Gandhian and a proclaimed admirer of Nehru and Indira Gandhi. I had helped him at the UN when he had come to New York in 1962 to present Zambia's case for independence. We met a number of times thereafter, particularly at the NAM and Commonwealth summits. He made very generous references to me in a letter he wrote to the Indian prime minister on my appointment. Desai's response was austere in the extreme. He wrote, 'I have read with interest your views on our new high commissioner. I hope Natwar Singh comes up to you expectations ...'

This was both graceless and tardy. I pointed this out in my letter to him saying that the least he could have done was to thank Kaunda for his friendly and warm words. Desai promptly replied on 23 May1978. It is not an epistle that does him any credit. 'I am surprised that you should attach so much importance to certificates from foreign dignitaries. They are entitled to their opinion as we are entitled to ours and they cannot expect us always to endorse their opinions without any reservation ...'

In other words, he was in so many words rejecting what President Kaunda had written about the Indian high commissioner. I pointed out that the Zambian president was not any ordinary foreign dignitary. This did me no good; a black mark was put against my name. But the incident that followed was even more bizarre and disagreeably hilarious.

Late in 1978 President Kaunda decided to send a high-powered delegation to India headed by the Zambian prime minister, including several cabinet ministers. Since 1947 it had been the established practice for heads of Indian missions to be in Delhi for presidential and prime ministerial visits. As I did not hear from the ministry I decided to accompany the delegation. From the narrow administrative point of view I should not have done so. But much more important was the political and diplomatic angle. The absence of the Indian high commissioner would have had two grave consequences. First, Africans are very protocol conscious; my absence would have been construed as our treating the Zambian visit as of no consequence. Second, it would have, in more ways than one, damaged my position vis-à-vis the Zambian government, among the media, the Indian community and the diplomatic corps.

My arrival in Delhi caused consternation and was considered a grave act of insubordination. I was asked to see the prime minister at 1, Safdarjung Road the next day at 8 a.m.

My wife drove me to the prime ministerial residence. It was bitterly cold. Fond memories of 1, Safdarjung Road came rushing to my mind. For nearly five years I had come here almost every day. Elegance and style had departed from the place now. I was conducted to Morarji Desai's room. It used to be Indira Gandhi's book-lined study. Now the room gave the impression of a dharamshala, with the PM's clothes hanging on a laundry line for drying.

Morarji Desai's opening words were, '*Aap begair bulaye aa gaye*.' (You have come without being asked to.) I said, 'I had been told that you wished to see me. I was asked to come at this time.' 'I am talking about your coming to Delhi without permission. You should have asked.' 'Sir, for twenty-nine years the well-established practice has been for heads of missions to be in India when a president or prime minister comes for a visit. I saw no reason to assume that a departure would be made in my case. Do you, sir, realize how badly it would have gone down with the Zambian leadership? Africans are very sensitive about such matters. Besides, did it not occur to anyone how adversely my position would have been affected in Lusaka if I were not in India during their prime minister's visit?'

There was an awkward silence followed by scarcely believable outrage. 'Why are you encouraging that terrorist, Nkomo?' Is this really happening or am I imagining things, I wondered. I replied, 'Sir, he is not a terrorist. He is a courageous and a highly respected freedom fighter.'

Continued Morarji Desai: 'I have been reading your reports from Zambia. They are not good.' Here the self-proclaimed Gandhian was skirting the truth. 'Sir, you must be the only person in South Block to read my dispatches. No one else looks at them. May I ask what is wrong with my reports?' 'They are too pro-Zambian,' was the reply.

This was truly mind-boggling. My response was without

any padding, 'I am in Lusaka to further strengthen, deepen and broaden our bilateral relations. Zambia is a very friendly country. President Kaunda greatly admires Gandhiji. Why should my reports be anti Zambia?' Pat came the reply, 'Kaunda is financing terrorists.'

I kept quiet. He knew nothing about Africa or Kaunda personally. He was undeniably trying to browbeat me. I gave him no comfort on this score.

As I was leaving, he asked, 'Where are you staying?'

'With my mother-in-law.'

'Where is your wife?'

'She is sitting in the car.'

'Ask her to come in.'

'Sir, that I will not do. I am not here on a social call.'

'Why are you arguing? Call her in.'

This was obviously an order, which the prime minister expected to be promptly obeyed. I decided not to oblige him. (This, I now realize, was quite improper.) As politely and respectfully as I could I told him that while he could order me on an official matter, he could not do so on personal issues.

The prime minister was rightly put out and said, 'You can go.'

My mother-in-law was at the time a Janata Party member of Rajya Sabha. She was close to Morarji Desai. He met her in Parliament later in the day and told her that her son-in-law was a very rude man. On that occasion, alas, I was.

3

A Progressive Conservative

In 1927 Mahatma Gandhi, referring to C. Rajagopalachari, had declared, 'I do say he is the only possible successor.' Rajaji was at the time a member of the Mahatma's inner circle. A public and serious falling out took place over the Cripps Mission in early 1942. Gandhiji called Cripps's proposals 'a post-dated cheque on a crashing bank.' Rajaji was supportive of the proposals. He was expelled from the Congress and did not participate in the Quit India Movement. It was then that Gandhiji declared, 'Not Rajaji, but Jawaharlal will be my successor.'

Nevertheless, on his release from jail in May 1944, Gandhiji sent for Rajaji for consultations in Panchgani. Thereafter C.R. did not look back and became governor general on the departure of Lord Mountbatten in June 1948.

Jawaharlal Nehru wanted C.R. to become president. Sardar Patel had not forgotten 1942 and opted for Rajendra Prasad. Patel had his way. Rajaji was called to Delhi to become home minister after the death of Sardar Patel. He also served as chief minister of Madras from 1952 to 1954. He later fell out with Nehru and launched the Swatantra Party, which for a short while made spectacular political inroads and sent several members to Parliament in the 1962 and 1967 Lok Sabha elections. Thereafter it withered away.

Rajaji came into my life unexpectedly. In October 1962 he led the Gandhi Peace Foundation delegation to press for a total ban on nuclear tests. After halts in Rome and London he arrived in New York. With him came R.R. Diwakar and B. Shiva Rao. The combined ages of the three added up to an impressive 223 years! I said to myself, 'Fancy sending three stretcher cases to meet John F. Kennedy.'

Rajaji's political relations with Nehru were strained, but their personal relations remained unimpaired. The prime minister had instructed the concerned embassies to extend all facilities to Rajaji. This was in keeping with Nehru's large-heartedness—private decencies could be extended to the political arena. We were, in those days, chronically short of foreign exchange. Wherever possible embassies were asked to put up Rajaji and his colleagues. I was told to play host to Rajaji in my two-bedroom apartment at 404 East, 66th Street.

This was the great man's first visit abroad. He was eighty-five years then. He arrived wearing a brown woollen *achkan* and, to my surprise, woollen trousers. These were soon discarded. It was back to dhoti.

I saw much of him during that period. He demonstrated with ease and grace how the rishis of ancient India lived. Here was a man of great wisdom, who never put on an act. His manners were exquisite, his speech gentle and soft. To me he was neither condescending nor patronizing. He was not given to making generalities or to verbal overkill. Language and thought had not become dehydrated. He was always punctual. His mind was complex but orderly, his curiosity childlike, his sarcastic wit unexpected.

Several distinguished people came to see him. These included Adlai Stevenson, the Democratic presidential candidate in 1952 and 1956, then the US ambassador to the UN; the UN secretary general U. Thant; Robert Oppenheimer, the great physicist; Louis Fischer, author of the best biography of Gandhiji, *The Life of Mahatma Gandhi*; Sir Zafarullah Khan, the president of the current session of the UN General Assembly; and Vincent Sheen, author of the book on Gandhi *Lead Kindly Light*. Sheen said to Rajaji, 'I am so glad Panditji sent you here. You should have come to Washington in 1950. I told the prime minister to send you as ambassador.' (In fact, Nehru had made this suggestion to Rajaji.)

I kept a diary during C.R.'s stay.

9 October 1962.

Rajaji in a relaxed, contemplative mood. I implored him to write his autobiography or dictate his memoir.

> C.R.: I know we have no sense of history, but does that really matter ultimately? After all, we do not know what Kalidas said to anyone. What he did and wrote is important.
>
> N.S.: If everyone took that view there would be no history. You have played such an active, at times decisive though controversial, role in recent Indian history that you owe it to the nation to leave behind your account of what

happened. After all Gandhiji and Pandit Nehru wrote autobiographies.

C.R.: Well, I had no time.

N.S.: Presumably your modesty prevents you from writing.

C.R.: No, I am not modest that way. I really had no time. I keep myself busy in so many ways.

N.S.: You must have had plenty of time when you were governor general.

C.R.: Yes! I did, but all that time was taken up in patching daily quarrels between the prime minister and the deputy prime minister. Pandit Nehru wanted me to stay in Delhi. The rest is well known.

N.S.: In 1953, I was secretary of the Cambridge Majlis and invited Lord Pethick-Lawrence (secretary of state for India in the Attlee government) to address the Majlis. Later I asked him, 'Which Indian leader impressed you the most?' and without hesitation he named you.

C.R.: Did he? I am glad to hear that. He was an excellent man. He wrote to me explaining why he had married again. Sir Stafford Cripps was a very impressive man but in the Cabinet Mission (1946) he played number two to Pethick-Lawrence …

The conversation then turned to Partition. To provoke him I said, 'Lord Mountbatten sold Partition to Panditji and Sardar Patel.'

C.R.: Now, let me tell you, Natwar Singh, I sold Partition to Mountbatten. The Attlee government had already made up its mind in that direction but did not know how to put it across in a concrete manner. Mountbatten asked me what he should do to break the impasse. I said Partition was the only answer. He first talked to Nehru and then to Patel. They had both seen what was going on and accepted reality.

N.S.: But Gandhiji was against Partition and held out till the very end. Why did he suddenly give in? It came as a great shock to someone young like me.

C.R.: Gandhiji was a great man but he too saw what was going on. He was a very disillusioned man. When he realized that we all accepted Partition, he said, 'If you all agree I will go along with you,' and after that he left Delhi.

10 October 1962.

C.R.: You should have come with me to the Columbia University meeting. The boys and girls there are very intelligent and asked me meaningful questions like what is dharma and karma. I told them dharma is universal duty and natural order.

Another day I asked him if in 1931 at the Karachi session of the AICC he was a party to the resolution on linguistic provinces. He was very forthright: he said he was, for 'political and propagandist reasons.' When he became home minister he had opposed the formation of the States Reorganization Commission, 'but no one listened to me.'

After he left New York I thought he would forget me. How wrong I was! For the next ten years we exchanged letters. So often he wrote in his own hand. His letters to me have been published. I end with quoting from the one he wrote on 24 November 1966 in which he reminisces about Indira Gandhi:

> I am not surprised you so much like the service under Smt. Indira Gandhi ... I can never forget the moving gesture of her affection as she came and received my daughter at the Delhi railway station, when I took her to Delhi from Bombay after she unexpectedly and cruelly lost her husband [Devadas Gandhi]. Indira Gandhi was at the station and led my daughter to the car like a sister ... This was August 1957, when I had already begun to openly and severely criticize Jawaharlalji.

4

Frontier Gandhi

The Forgotten Hero

The first time I set foot on Afghan soil was in September 1969 when I was a member of Indira Gandhi's delegation. At the time Indo-Afghan relations were cordial and close. There was not a cloud in the Afghan sky.

Apart from the formal aspect of the visit, the prime minister was to meet Khan Abdul Ghaffar Khan, the Frontier Gandhi. This was to be the highlight of her trip.

Bloodletting comes to the Pathan with fatal ease. Khan Abdul Ghaffar Khan achieved the impossible. Inspired by Gandhiji, he led a non-violent movement in the North West Frontier Province during the freedom struggle. Non-violence is alien to the Afghan/Pathan character. Badshah Khan's Khudai Khidmatgars embraced non-violence. It was a unique conversion. Khan spent several months at Sevagram in the 1930s; he also met Tagore at Shantiniketan.

Four Congress leaders opposed the partition of India: Gandhiji, Khan Abdul Ghaffar Khan, Jayaprakash Narayan and Ram Manohar Lohia. Maulana Abul Kalam Azad too was against Partition, but in his own way. The Congress Working Committee met on 31 May and on 2 and 3 June 1947. At these meetings the momentous decision was taken to accept Partition. The Frontier Gandhi felt betrayed. He had been imprisoned by the British several times. The same fate awaited him in Pakistan. In all, Khan Abdul Ghaffar Khan, like Nelson Mandela, spent twenty-seven years in prison. His was a life of struggle, sacrifice, service, suffering and sorrow. At the same time, an inspiring life.

At the reception given by Ashok Mehta, the Indian ambassador to Afghanistan, for the prime minister, Badshah Khan, who was living in Kabul, was naturally invited. Mrs Gandhi was meeting him after twenty-two years. She introduced Rajiv and Sonia Gandhi to him. The Frontier Gandhi, 6'5", embraced Rajiv Gandhi telling him that he had held him in his arms when he was two years old. The thirty-five-year young Rajiv Gandhi gave a blushy smile.

Later I went to the house where Badshah Khan was staying. It was dinner time. He and his companions were dipping their naans in a large bowl full of meat and some vegetables. They all looked like figures from the Old Testament. All were sitting on the floor. I was invited to join in the repast. This I did with some hesitation. During the meal I informed Badshah Khan of Mrs Gandhi's wish to come to meet him at his convenience. He would have none of it. He would go to see her. He chose the time. Next day at 4 p.m. at the State House.

I was to receive him in the porch. I was a few seconds late. He was already walking up the staircase when I got there.

In a clear voice he admonished me in chaste Urdu: '*Aapko wakth per aana chahiye tha.*' All I could do was apologize sheepishly. His remarkable punctuality made a captivating impression on me. At his meeting with the prime minister it was agreed that he would come to Delhi for Mahatma Gandhi's centenary on 2 October 1969.

Before I write about Badshah Khan's memorable sojourn in Delhi, I cannot resist mentioning the following episode.

One afternoon the PM's schedule being not too demanding, she said she would like to go for a drive. About a couple of miles out of Kabul she noticed a green patch on the shoulder of a hill. We were told that it was the resting place of Emperor Babur. She expressed her desire to see it. So up the hill we drove, to the dismay of our Afghan escorts, because there would be no one there to receive her. What at one time must have been an attractive garden-cum-graveyard was now an overgrown jungle. Obviously Babur did not mean much to the Afghans. It took a while to locate the grave. The PM stood there for a few moments in silence. I stood a couple of feet behind her. 'We have had our brush with history,' she remarked. I said, 'I have had two.' 'What do you mean?' I replied, 'To pay respect to Babur is itself an occasion. To do so in the company of Indira Gandhi is the rarest of privileges.'

Khan Abdul Ghaffar Khan was coming to India after twenty-two years. His arrival aroused much interest. He was among the very few Gandhians who were still alive. He emerged from the plane with a lathi—at the end of it was a little bundle containing his worldly goods. He got a tumultuous welcome. Indira Gandhi and Jayaprakash Narayan received him. He was to be driven in an open car with the PM sitting next to him. Jayaprakash Narayan made an attempt to get in the car. The PM was not keen on it. When a security officer tried to prevent him from getting into the car, the normally serene JP flared up. I, to avoid an unseemly incident, asked the security man to let go. JP got into the car.

A day or two after Badshah Khan's arrival, communal riots broke out in several parts of the country. He announced a three-day fast. Immediately the riots stopped. He then made a statement which touched the hearts of his erstwhile countrymen, 'I have considered myself a part of you and you as a part of me.' At other times, he was severally critical of certain aspects of our national life. Rebuttal was out of the question. The Frontier Gandhi was a law unto himself. In an hour-long speech on the lawns of Teen Murti House, not once did he mention Jawaharlal Nehru's name.

Badshah Khan again came to India in December 1985 for the Congress centenary celebrations held in Bombay. The last time was in 1987 for treatment. He was awarded the Bharat Ratna. The first non-Indian so honoured.

He passed away on 20 January 1988. He was ninety-eight. Rajiv Gandhi attended his funeral in Jalalabad. A great and noble soul had departed.

5

A False Alarm

The third Non-Aligned Movement (NAM) summit was held in Lusaka, Zambia, early in September 1970. Prime Minister Indira Gandhi was the star attraction along with Marshal Tito of Yugoslavia.

In those far-off, less hectic and less demanding days, the prime minister travelled on commercial airlines. The only special concession the airline would make was to leave the seat next to her vacant, so that she could keep her books, files and papers on it.

At the Santa Cruz airport in Bombay the PM was seen off by the governor, the chief minister and J.R.D. Tata. A smooth take off. The Arabian Sea was glistening, monsoon clouds thick but not threatening. Besides the PM, P.N. Haksar, her principal secretary, and K.B. Lal, secretary of commerce, sat in the first class. The rest of us were chatting away in the economy class. About half an hour after take off, B.L. Joshi (now governor of Uttar Pradesh), the PM's security officer, was called to the cockpit. He returned, looking more than anxious, and whispered in my ear, 'Natwar Singhji, the pilot has just told me that one of the passengers is carrying a bomb.' A bomb on Indira Gandhi's plane! I got up and informed the PM. She kept reading. Then to my astonishment she said, 'It's a hoax. Let's keep going.' Cool. Very cool. Most impressive. Also most disconcerting. I went to P.N. Haksar who asked, 'Have you told her?' 'Yes, I have.' 'What did she say?' 'It's a hoax. Let's keep going.' Haksar said nothing for a few moments. Then came this unambiguous command, 'Natwar, tell the PM that on matters concerning her security the deciding authority is her secretary. We are flying back to Bombay.' I did as I was told. 'Do what you like' was Mrs Gandhi's dismissive remark. The plane turned around, dumping most of the petrol in the Arabian Sea. A few minutes before landing the pilot told Joshi that the man with the bomb was a Patel. Vital additional information was also passed on. According to records no less than nineteen Patels were on the plane. While we were still in the air, All India Radio had announced that the prime minister was returning to Bombay on account of a passenger carrying a bomb. I later learnt that on hearing this sensational news, my wife had frantically telephoned Mrs Haksar, who was quite oblivious to it.

The fire brigade was in attendance when we landed. All baggage was unloaded. The nineteen Patels were all but stripped. No bomb. Only undeclared foreign currency! The search took more than two hours. There was no point in going to the Raj Bhavan in the short time we had before the next flight. The PM rested in her lounge and was entertained by J.R.D. Tata, who was well known as a storehouse of jokes—risque ones included. For the PM only the vegetarian ones. I remember J.R.D. regaling her with stories about a pilot named Screwallah.

The PM afterwards walked up to a bookstall, browsed through several volumes and bought *Airport* by Arthur Hailey. The bookshop owner refused to accept payment, but was eventually persuaded.

We took off for Nairobi and then on to Lusaka. The Zambian president, Kenneth Kaunda, and Indira Gandhi felt comfortable in each other's company. She was seven years older than him and he respected her as an elder, not only as the prime minister of a great country.

The luminaries of the summit, besides Indira Gandhi and Tito, were Emperor of Ethiopia Haile Selassie, President Julius Nyerere of Tanzania, Kenneth Kaunda, Archbishop Makarios of Cyprus, and Forbes Burnham of Guyana. Since the summit was being held in a southern African country, South Africa, South-West Africa (now Namibia), Angola, Mozambique and Southern Rhodesia (now Zimbabwe) figured prominently there. South Africa was the home of apartheid. South-West Africa was a trust territory under South Africa. Angola and Mozambique were under the yoke of Portugal. Southern Rhodesia's racist government under Ian Smith had declared unilateral independence.

When the draft final statement was being made ready, the Afghan PM added two lines supporting the Turkish position on Cyprus. Archbishop Makarios of Cyprus said he could not accept this amendment. He needed Indira Gandhi's help. He could not go back to Cyprus unless this amendment was rejected. Mrs Gandhi asked me to make a request to Marshal Tito, President Nyerere, President Kaunda, the host and the archbishop. These four leaders persuaded the Afghan PM to withdraw his amendment which he reluctantly did. Indira Gandhi had defused a situation which could have lead to a serious crisis at the summit.

Leaders from NAM countries are allergic to short speeches. The docility with which people in non-aligned countries suffer long and cliché-ridden speeches is extraordinary. Indira Gandhi was not given to rhetorical inflation or prolixity. So often it is said that she did not write her own speeches. In Lusaka I was with her for three days and saw her composing her speech. I have preserved her handwritten notes. These ran into four pages. Her speech, delivered on 9 September 1970, set the tone of the summit. She said:

> Here in Lusaka we can feel the ebb and flow of the continuing battle against remnants of colonialism in Angola and Mozambique. We can feel the vibrations of the struggle against the minority government in Zimbabwe and the apartheid policies of the racist regimes in the Union of South Africa, and the strivings of the national movements in Namibia and in Guinea Bissau ... From the beginning, there has been no lack of inquisitions, which looked upon non-alignment as heresy and distorted its meaning. Many believed it would not work. But we can answer back in the spirit of the famous words of Galileo, 'And yet, it moves!'

She continued, 'We are in no camp and in no military alliance. The only camp we would like to be in is the camp of peace, which should include as many countries as possible.'

Indira Gandhi's contribution to the success of the summit was tremendous.

6

A Teddy Bear and a Slipped Disc

My son Jagat was born on 28 August 1968. The same day Indira Gandhi sent me a handwritten letter:

> Dear Natwar,
>
> As soon as I heard the good news from the Secretary, I tried to speak to you on the phone, but for some reason could not get through.
>
> Hearty congratulations to you both and blessings to the little one. May he grow up to be a source of joy and pride to you.
>
> With good wishes,
> Indira Gandhi

Indira Gandhi inspired in me a lasting affection and respect, almost verging on veneration. I have a deep sense of gratitude, as I owe her more than I can say. Possibly more than I know. History has not done justice to her. She was endowed with a radiant persona: charming, elegant, stylish, beautiful. What savoir faire, what composure! Yet she has been depicted as severe, solemn, stern, shifty, scheming. Seldom is it conceded that she was a sparkling human being, a caring humanist, a voracious reader and lover of books, with wide-ranging non-political interests, who enjoyed the company of authors, artists, poets and painters and, above all, she had a sense of humour.

Those who had worked under her and with her were truly fortunate. Our experience was far more exciting and richer than those whom fortune had not favoured with such an opportunity. My life would have been the poorer, less stimulating and with a restricted vision, but for her.

On 27 January 1970, I sent her a brief note from Patiala, where I was staying with my in-laws:

> Having failed to solve the problem of addressing you (Dear Madam, Dear Mrs Gandhi, Dear Shrimati Gandhi, Dear PM, etc.) I have decided to send this in note form.
>
> It is now over two weeks that I have been condemned to lie flat on my back on a hard wooden bed as a result of a slipped disc. On the 11th, I bent down to give my son, Jagat, his teddy bear, when it happened. I would have thought that middle age would arrive with a little more ceremony and a little less pain. What makes it worse is being away from Delhi during these days. What makes it intolerable is that I have literally to take it lying down.
>
> My principal pastime is to stare at the ceiling without having the least desire to paint it. I have enjoyed reading John Gunther's latest book, *Twelve Cities*—racy, absorbing and loaded with memorable trivia. I could hardly recommend it to the PM in the week preceding the

> budget, but I do strongly recommend a gripping essay by Zbigniew Brzezinski, 'Technical Age'. His view is that the future would be shaped by technology and electronics. To describe this revolutionary transformation, he has coined the phrase, 'Technocratic Age'.

I did not expect a reply. But reply she did. It was a caring, light-hearted epistle that she wrote to me on 30 January.

> Dear Natwar,
>
> I knew you were on leave but I had no idea it was caused by physical incapacity to turn up. I know how painful a slipped disc can be. You have all my sympathy—however it is giving you time to ruminate on the past, present and the future and this is something which we all need from time to time. You can imagine how life in Delhi is when one is facing explosive issues and VIPs during the Republic week. I am off on tour tomorrow morning.
>
> Do you remember when the same thing happened to K.P.S. Menon? He had to stand in a very artistic Ajanta pose for quite sometime. Now you know the perils of fatherhood!
>
> With every good wish for a complete recovery.

A busy prime minister finding time to write to an official in her secretariat shows what a thoughtful and gracious person she was.

Here I cannot resist the temptation to recall three other incidents.

One of my most pleasant duties was to sit next to the PM in her car—an Ambassador. On her fiftieth birthday she was at Palam Airport to receive the president of Czechoslovakia. On the drive to the airport I asked her how she felt about reaching the half-century (it was later that I learnt that one should never forget the birthday of a lady but always forget her age). She told me a story.

> There was a young woman who did not want to be thirty. At midnight of 29–30 she hid under her bed. The next morning her husband looked everywhere for his wife to congratulate her on her thirtieth. Finally he located her under the bed. 'Honey, what's the matter. Why are you hiding under the bed?' She replied in a tearful tone, 'Darling, I don't want to be thirty.'
>
> Then she added, 'After thirty I have not bothered to remember my age.'

For visiting heads of state a reception used to be organized at the Diwan-i-Aam at the Red Fort, even if the temperature was 10°C in winter or 45°C in summer. President Gamal Abded Nasser too was honoured at the Red Fort. The function began with the national anthem of the guest country played by an army band. Both President Nasser and Mrs Gandhi stood up when the band began to play. As soon as the ritual was over, the Egyptian leader leaned towards the PM and whispered something to her. I was sitting behind them. She turned to me and said, 'Nasser just told me that the band played the anthem of King Farouk.' He had been deposed in 1952 by the army colonels. Nasser was one of them. Mercifully, no one else in the audience was any the wiser. Heads did not roll, but the PM asked me to make sure that such an error did not occur again. It did not.

One day in the winter of 1967 she said to me, 'Natwar, I am without a cook. Can you find one for me?' I said I would ask my father-in-law if he could send one from Patiala. The cook arrived. I took him to 1, Safdarjung Road and informed the PM. The man started work in the kitchen.

Three days later, G.C. Dutt, joint secretary of the Intelligence Bureau, came to see me. He was in great distress. 'Natwar Singhji, how could you do this? You never told me that you had sent a cook to prepare the PM's meals. I am in charge of her security.' He also said that I surely knew that all employees working at 1, Safdarjung Road, had to have his clearance. He was right. I should have told him first. But those were such carefree days that security concerns had not reached the proportions they have today. I apologized to Dutt. When I told the PM about Dutt rightly upbraiding me, she just smiled. The cook was removed. I had learnt a lesson.

7

An Encounter with Robert Mugabe

On 24 January 1980 Indira Gandhi took on the mantle of prime ministership for the second time. Hers was a heroic and triumphant comeback. A few days later R.K. Dhawan, the PM's personal assistant, was on the phone, 'Indiraji will speak to you.' She did. She asked how I was and when I would be coming to Delhi. I was surprised and touched. She had a million tasks to perform, yet she found time to call me in Lusaka, Zambia.

The news got around and the Ministry of External Affairs immediately rediscovered me! Before leaving for Delhi I paid a visit to Salisbury (current name Harare), the capital city of Zimbabwe, to get in touch with Robert Mugabe. His party, the Zimbabwe African National Union (ZANU), had handsomely won the recent elections. India had backed Joshua Nkomo and his Zimbabwe African People's Union (ZAPU). For the first time in our dealings with African leaders, struggling against colonial rule, we had backed the wrong horse. I had been in regular touch with Nkomo, whose headquarters were in Lusaka. Mugabe, after his ten-year imprisonment as a political prisoner in Rhodesia, had shifted to Beira in Mozambique.

He had outsmarted his senior, Nkomo, whom we could not abandon. But Mugabe had to be contacted. Locating the ZANU leader was hard work. We had withdrawn our diplomats from Southern Rhodesia in the 1950s on account of its racial policies. When it became clear that the independence of the colony was around the African bush, we sent Arif Qamrain, our first secretary in the high commission in London, to Salisbury. He arrived there on 26 January 1980. He had worked with me when I was serving as ambassador in Warsaw, Poland. His languid manner was deceptive. He was not given to verbal excess and steered clear of sycophancy.

On arrival in Salisbury I asked Arif to arrange for me to meet the future prime minister of Zimbabwe. Easier said than done. Mugabe's whereabouts were not known. There was apparently some danger to his life. He was a courageous man, who so far had lived dangerously. At the same time, he thought it prudent not to expose himself. Arif Qamrain, in a benign way, 'infiltrated' the Indian community in the Rhodesian capital. He got hold of Suman Mehta, an activist and a member of ZAPU. Like an astute politician he had friends in ZANU as well. He said to Arif that he would try to arrange a meeting between me and Mugabe but could not give any assurance. All I could do meanwhile was cool my heels. Finally, Mehta came up with encouraging news. Mugabe might see me and Arif late at night at an undisclosed location. We arrived at a point after which Arif had to abandon his car. We piled into Mehta's vehicle. In the pitch dark the driver took a roundabout route to beat the white louts. We finally halted in front of a modest building. There, in an ill-lit room, Robert Mugabe was seated on a low chair wrapped in a blanket—it was a cold night.

After giving him Prime Minister Indira Gandhi's greetings and good wishes, I said how much we admired his valiant struggle against the colonialists and racists, and how great an honour it was to meet one of Africa's great sons, etc. My sugared diplomatic platitudes came out drip by drip. Mugabe knew only too well that we had backed his rival. His response was terse and polite. He thanked India and asked me to convey his regards to Mrs Gandhi. I tremulously enquired if invitations for the Zimbabwean independence day celebrations on 18 April had been sent out to heads of state and heads of government. He said that all that was being done by the governor, Sir Christopher Soames, who was the son-in-law of Winston Churchill and a minor Tory figure.

I had, in Lusaka, heard that the British did not want 18 April to be a huge and prolonged celebration. With that in mind I said to Mugabe that India was the first country to get rid of the colonialists. Zimbabwe would be the last. It was therefore appropriate that the occasion be celebrated in a befitting and memorable manner. He seemed to approve. Before leaving I asked, 'Sir, could I tell Mrs Gandhi how much you are looking forward to greeting her in an independent Zimbabwe?' 'Of course, of course, do tell her. I admire her and her great father,' he replied.

President Mugabe continues to be in power but after some controversial decisions on land reform and a disputed presidential election he is internationally isolated.

Indira Gandhi landed in Harare on 17 April. She stayed at the Monomotapa Hotel. I was a part of her entourage which also included P.V. Narasimha Rao. The high and mighty leaders of the world had all turned up in large numbers. Britain sent Prince Charles to bring down the colonial curtain. The UN secretary general Kurt Waldheim was very prominent among the gathering. Indira Gandhi was the high-voltage star and a much sought-after leader. Two meetings I recall vividly.

President Zia-ul-Haq of Pakistan sent a message to the prime minister asking when he could call on her. Protocol required that she as head of government call on him, a head of state. This was conveyed to him. He would have none of it. Before General Zia arrived the PM asked me, 'What should I say to him?' My answer was, 'That depends on the kind of relations we wish to have with Pakistan.' They certainly needed restructuring after the Janata experiment (1977–80). She had, soon after taking over as PM, sent Swaran Singh to Islamabad to talk to Zia. I suggested she might use that visit as a starting point.

The meeting turned out to be a non-event except for the photographers. General Zia appeared a bit awed. One of his observations elicited a shattering put down—'They call me a dictator and you a democrat.' Zia presented Indira Gandhi an illustrated coffee-table book on Pakistan. When she later looked at it, she was far from amused. The general had been knowingly crude. The map in the book showed the whole of Kashmir as a part of Pakistan. I returned the book to the Pakistan foreign office.

Among others who came to see her was the old warhorse W. Averell Harriman, the American diplomat and politician. I had warned her that Harriman was hard of hearing. So she raised her voice a notch or two. He was followed by Peter Shore, the British Labour MP, who had also been a cabinet minister. He was taken aback when he heard Mrs Gandhi speaking to him in an unusually loud voice. I discreetly passed a slip to her, 'Peter is *not* deaf.' She explained to him that she had just been speaking to Harriman who 'is quite deaf and I had to raise my voice'. Shore heaved a sigh of relief.

8

Dr Zakir Hussain's Death and Beyond

The year 1969 was a crucial one for Prime Minister Indira Gandhi. Momentous events followed one after another. President Zakir Hussain's unexpected death on 3 May 1969 caused a politic tsunami of gigantic proportions. The prime minister was away in Jodhpur. The president's personal physician telephoned me to give the news. P.N. Haksar, Mrs Gandhi's secretary, and I rushed to Rashtrapati Bhavan. V.V. Giri, the vice-president, took the oath as acting president.

Who should succeed Dr Zakir Hussain? The matter caused a constitutional and political earthquake. Giri at the time had no takers. The syndicate chose the speaker of the Lok Sabha, N. Sanjiva Reddy, as its candidate. The prime minister remained non-committal. Keeping her cool she left for official tours to Japan and Indonesia. I was also a part of the entourage. She kept herself informed of developments at home. The syndicate became a den of plotters. At the meetings of the parliamentary board of the Congress, she was all but 'humiliated'. She skipped one of the meetings of the working committee.

She dictated a few 'stray thoughts'. The courier was the faithful Fakhruddin Ahmed (he later became a rubber stamp *rashtrapati*). The stray notes subtly carried an ideological message. Deftly the personal element was jettisoned. Her next move was bold and devastating. She divested Morarji Desai of his finance portfolio, and requested him to continue as deputy prime minister. He was shocked and resigned. Her next act was a masterstroke. On 18 July 1969 she had an ordinance passed, nationalizing fourteen leading commercial banks. This move was vastly popular with a majority of the people and was enthusiastically welcomed by the 'young Turks'.

Mrs Gandhi eventually decided to put up V.V. Giri as her candidate. The syndicate selected Sanjiva Reddy. The die was cast. Giri resigned as vice-president on 18 July 1969. Chief Justice M. Hidayatullah was sworn in as acting president. The pressures on Indira Gandhi were heavy and unrelenting. She was not overwhelmed; neither did she lose her nerve.

It was at this stage that I got indirectly drawn into the historic machinations. The Congress parliamentary party had split. My mother-in-law, Maharani Mohinder Kaur of Patiala, joined the Morarji faction in the Lok Sabha. At one time she and Indira Gandhi had been close friends. After her husband, Feroze Gandhi's death, in September 1960, at the age of forty-eight, Indiraji had spent several weeks in Chail, Himachal Pradesh, as a personal guest of the maharani. It soon became evident that the presidential election was going to be an uncomfortably close one. Every single vote of the MPs was of critical importance. The stakes could not be higher. (A distraction was provided by President Nixon, who arrived in Delhi on 31 July 1969 for a twenty-four-hour stay. It was not a memorable visit.)

One day the dogged, unflappable and deceptively unconcerned Sardar Swaran Singh asked me to meet him. 'Natwar, I am talking to you man to man, not as a cabinet minister. You must speak to Maharani Sahiba and request her not to side with Morarji Desai. She has known Indiraji much longer than Morarji bhai.' I was a middle-level official in the PM's secretariat, and a minor player in the Great Game. I was perplexed; I said nothing.

A day or two later, K.K. Shah, the information and broadcasting minister, collared me in Parliament. He himself came from a minor princely state in Gujarat. He was not a political heavyweight but had not deserted Indira Gandhi. For a Gujarati to cross swords with Morarji bhai was not a painless exercise. Shah was not devoid of sophistication either. I listened, saying nothing. My unease increased.

I shall not name the third minister's name, as he is still with us. He was forceful and had the temerity to imply that my mother-in-law's betrayal would affect me adversely. My instinct was to reply indignantly, but good sense prevailed and I kept my cool.

Nevertheless, by now, I had had enough of the not-so-gentle ministerial pressurizing. I went straight to Parliament to meet the prime minister. She was in the Lok Sabha. I sent her a brief note saying that I was very upset and must see her. I waited in the private secretary's room. The PM arrived at her office sooner than I expected. 'What's bothering you, Natwar?' I repeated to her what the three worthies had asked me to do. 'Madam, I am in your secretariat as an officer of the Indian Foreign Service, and not as the son-in-law of the Patialas. I do not discuss politics with my mother-in-law and have no desire to do so. I do very much mind being harassed in this manner. I am very upset.' She heard me out. Having unburdened myself I left her room with a lighter heart if not a spring in my steps.

This is what followed. She spoke to all three of her cabinet colleagues individually. She asked them to 'Keep Natwar out of this. My staff perform their duties to my entire satisfaction. This includes Natwar.' She would have been entirely justified to have been dismissive of my tantrum. She was not. What a wonderful example of a prime minister protecting even a junior member of her staff!

PS: Before the presidential election, the PM instructed her staff to prepare two speeches: one, if Giri was elected; the second, if he was defeated. 'I shall sit in the Opposition if necessary,' she had declared. Both texts were ready in time. V.V. Giri got through by the skin of his teeth. The prime minister delivered the first speech.

9

Princes, Privileges and Privy Purses

Among the overwhelming problems confronting the Central government after 15 August 1947 was that of princely India, consisting of about six hundred states. Hyderabad and Kashmir were nearly the size of France; though some of the others were minuscule. Constitutionally, the princely states were not a part of British India, nor were they British subjects. The British parliament had no power to legislate for these states. The crown's relationship with the princes was mediated by the governor general in council. The viceroy looked after British India. The remarkable fact was that the governor general and the viceroy were one and the same person. Trust imperial Britain to come up with so adroit a formula. It worked for almost a century. The governor general represented the paramount power, while paramountcy remained a vague concept.

On 25 July 1947, Lord Mountbatten addressed the Chamber of Princes, whose chancellor was my father-in-law, the Maharaja of Patiala. He told his colourful audience that after 15 August 1947 they could no longer count on the British crown to help them. They would have the option to sign the Instrument of Accession prepared by the Ministry of States under Sardar Vallabhbhai Patel. Most signed. Maharaja Hari Singh of Kashmir did so only after Pakistan attacked his state in October. His Exalted Highness the Nizam fell in line only in mid-1948, after India sent in troops to Hyderabad.

This, somewhat prolix, introduction is necessary to comprehend what followed. The Instrument of Accession, in fact, had stripped the maharajas and nawabs of real power but not of pomp and circumstance. They were assured tax-free privy-purse privileges (the nizam was to get fifty lakh annually); they could not be taken to court; their titles they retained; palaces, red number plates, etc. were not to be touched. Pandit Nehru and Sardar Patel had achieved a mini miracle. The balkanization of India was avoided. Sardar Patel outdid Otto von Bismarck, the German chancellor who united Germany in the latter half of the nineteenth century.

By the mid-1960s the national mood was changing on the privy-purse issue. The Swatantra Party founded by C. Rajagopalachari did well in the 1967 elections. It was a rightist outfit and several princes became its members. The young Turks in the Congress—Chandra Shekhar, Krishna Kant, Chandrajit Yadav—at the All India Congress Committee (AICC) meeting in Simla in the summer of 1967 succeeded in passing a resolution demanding the abolition of the privy purses and privileges of the princes. Not many

AICC members were present when the resolution was passed. Prime Minister Indira Gandhi was not able to attend the meeting, and this development took her by surprise.

The Swatantra Party objected to the abolition of the privy purses saying it went against the assurances given by Sardar Patel earlier. Some of the princes, overestimating their influence, decided to take on the government. In the process they overplayed their hand. An outfit called the Concord of Princes was floated. By mid-1970 it was clear that the Concord wished for a confrontation. The government did not. Mrs Gandhi wrote to the princes (I drafted the letter) appealing to their good sense. Also, cautioning them that it was unwise to ignore 'the temper of the times'.

Often, Indira Gandhi is accused of giving a raw deal to the princes. This is untrue. The facts are as follows: Though she kept herself fully informed she had entrusted the task of dealing with the privy-purse issue to the following people: Home Minister Y.B. Chavan, Home Secretary L.P. Singh, Minister of State in the Home Ministry K.C. Pant, Secretary to the Rashtrapati Nagendra Singh, who was the younger brother of the Maharaja of Dungarpur, and myself. The princes could not have got so understanding and well-intentioned a group. I personally took several of the rulers to meet the prime minister. She also met representatives from the Concord: Fatehsinhrao Gaekwad of Baroda, Begum Sahiba of Bhopal and the Maharaja of Dhrangadhra. They blew it. I could scarcely believe that such were the people selected to espouse a lost cause. The state of Dhrangadhra cannot be located on most maps—yet the raja's stilted accent (he had been to Oxford) and pompous manner irritated one and all. Dr Karan Singh was a very prominent prince and a member of Indira Gandhi's cabinet—he fully supported the government of which he was proud to be a part. The Concord was unwise to reject Indira Gandhi's more than generous offer. I shall mention only one item: the government offered a generous package—the amount due over ten years as privy purse in a lump sum to each ruler. By the end of July 1970 it was clear that a showdown was inevitable in spite of the government having played fair.

Finally, the government moved the 24th Constitution Amendment Bill (abolition of privy purses and princely privileges) in the Lok Sabha. It was carried by 339 to 154 votes. I was sitting in the official gallery of the Rajya Sabha when the bill was put to vote. It was, to my horror, rejected by one vote. That very night a presidential ordinance was passed de-recognizing the princes. Next morning Indira Gandhi left for Mauritius. I, too, with her.

PS: The Concord challenged the ordinance in the Supreme Court, which ruled against it. The princes were impoverished. Their lawyers were enriched. A striking case of *vinaash kale vipreet buddhi* …

10

The Legacy of Nehru

In 1960 Jawaharlal Nehru looked as if he would live for another twenty years. Fate decreed otherwise. The 1962 conflict with China took a grievous toll on him. It was the greatest political tragedy of his life. He had, in good faith, invested far too much in his policy towards the People's Republic of China. He felt let down. That was an Oxbridge response. He was a wounded lion who could not shed his anguish. Gone were the élan, the nonchalance, the superhuman energy, the capacity to work eighteen hours a day. An acute melancholy overcame this most lovable of human beings. A week before his death, he said at a press conference that his life was not coming to an end so soon. Death came on 27 May 1964. I wept.

The UN Security Council met that very day to pay homage. Adlai Stevenson, the US ambassador to the UN, paid a deeply moving tribute. During his extensive 1949 tour of the United States, Nehru had met Stevenson in Chicago. Stevenson was then the governor of Illinois. Welcoming Nehru he had said:

> Only a tiny handful of men have influenced the implacable forces of our times. To this small company of the truly great Pandit Jawaharlal Nehru belongs. We pay our homage, not just because he is the prime minister of India, but because he is a great and good man ... He was one of God's great creations in our time. His monument is his nation and his dream of freedom and ever-expanding well-being for all men.

Jawaharlal Nehru summoned the stars to his table. He never betrayed himself and thus avoided spiritual destruction. Within a few days of his demise, I decided to write to Nehru's American publishers, John Day Company, asking whether they would be interested in publishing a volume of tributes to the great leader which I would edit. Their response was encouraging. My book on E.M. Forster had been a literary success without being a financial disaster, so I was not wholly unknown to a section of the New York publishing community. I was also reviewing books for the *Saturday Review* and *The New York Times Book Review*.

I sent Richard Walsh, the owner of John Day, a list of Nehru's contemporaries and admirers whom I intended to write to. From a list of twenty only three conveyed their inability to contribute. The American economist Kenneth Galbraith came up with a feeble excuse. President D. Eisenhower's office wrote that I could consult the Eisenhower Papers. President Harry S. Truman wrote a disarming letter.

Harry S. Truman
Independence,
Missouri 64050

Dear Mr Natwar Singh,

In reply to your letter, my recent mishap has caused me to lose contact with my correspondents until my return to office several days ago.

I wish that it was possible for me to act upon your request to write a tribute to the late Prime Minister Nehru, for it is something that I would very much want to do, but under present circumstances, I am well advised to forego all such undertakings until I resume my full working schedule.

Yours sincerely,
Harry S. Truman

Four Nobel laureates obliged: Pearls S. Buck, Martin Luther King, Jr, Linus Pauling and Bertrand Russell. King gave me and Walsh some anxious moments. His article did not reach me till the end of February 1965. The book was to appear on 27 May 1965, the first anniversary of Nehru's death.

The reason for the delay was his being in and out of jail. In those grim days prison life in the southern states of America was for blacks a very disgraceful experience. He wrote about Nehru with discernment and passion while in jail in Selma, Alabama: 'Even though his physical presence is gone, his spiritual influence retains a living force … Nehru's example in daring to believe and act for peaceful coexistence gives mankind its most glowing hope … Nehru sits unseen but is felt at all council tables.'

Bertrand Russell and Jawaharlal Nehru did not always agree with each other but mutual regard was never abandoned. Russell got the essentials of Nehru's vision spot on: 'Every conceivable argument has been available to tempt Mr Nehru to forego democratic institutions in India ... Had Nehru made this decision, it is doubtful that the rule of law or representative institutions would have any chance among emergent nations. To the extent they do is the achievement of Nehru.'

Pearl Buck wrote of Nehru's literary excellence: 'I know that had our times been more peaceful he could have found a high career as a creative writer, for his style of writing is distinguished and his imagination alive and quick ... I am grateful for the few important books he wrote, all of them basic in their importance.'

Writer Raja Rao's piece could only have been written by an erudite south Indian Brahmin. It is a confluence of the religious, the mystical, the philosophical and the esoteric. In late 1935 Nehru was living in Badenweiler, in the Black Forest in Germany, where his wife, Kamala, was receiving treatment for tuberculosis. Raja Rao traced him there. Nehru said to Raja Rao, 'Romain Rolland spoke to me about you.' Rolland had won the Nobel Prize for Literature in 1915; he had also written biographies of Gandhi and Vivekananda. He knew Tagore and Gandhi and through them Jawaharlal Nehru.

When Raja told Nehru that he had spent a year at Aligarh, Nehru tested his Urdu.

J.N.: What's 'afternoon' in Deccani Urdu?

R.R.: *Do-pahar.*

J.N.: And 'late afternoon'?

R.R.: Oh, that I'm afraid I do not remember.

J.N.: *Teesre-pahar.*

The tutorial had much more, but I shall leave it out. The Urdu lesson greatly amused Nehru's sick wife.

The historian Arnold J. Toynbee was captivated by Nehru. 'Here was a human being who could win one's heart and keep it,' he said.

I was keen to get a Russian to join the list of contributors to the volume. I wrote to the Soviet writer Ilya Ehrenburg through our embassy in Moscow. Ehrenburg was a man of letters and trusted by the Soviets. He excelled in tightrope walking. His books were widely read and were not censored. His *The Thaw* was the first hint that de-Stalinization was round the corner. Ehrenburg admired Nehru as a sensitive humanist, and called him 'a miraculous alloy of ages, cultures and ideologies'.

My own homage was excessively emotional, lachrymal even. At that time my critical faculties had atrophied.

11

Nehru's Sisters

Jawaharlal Nehru had two sisters: Vijayalakshmi Pandit was eleven years younger than him; Krishna Hutheesing, eighteen years. I got to know the latter in July 1944 when I shifted from the overtly aristocratic and feudal ambience of Mayo College, Ajmer, to Scindia School, Gwalior. Harsh and Ajit Hutheesing, her two sons, also joined the school the same year. All three of us were placed in Jayaji House, one of the six residential houses at the school.

When I joined the IFS I realized that my closeness to Krishna Hutheesing was known to her elder sister and not approved. In 1960 the rumour in the ministry was that I was being posted to London as private secretary to the high commissioner, Vijayalakshmi Pandit. I knew nothing about it till I received a letter from Krishna Masi (as I now called her) dated 2 April. She was staying with her sister at 9, Kensington Palace Gardens, the palatial residence of the high commissioner. She was obviously privy to what I was not:

Natwar dear,

Heard the glad tidings that you have been 'promoted'! Congratulations. It's a pity you will come here after I've returned. Any how Harsh will be here or in Cambridge.

Saw Forster's play (*A Passage to India*)—wasn't too good but seems to be going down well with the English public. My sister says that the fact an English woman was raped in a beautiful cave excites the imagination of all the frustrated people here.

Love,
Masi.

PS:

You should get married before you come on this assignment—so the elders think.

There was another line: 'For someone who is coming here, it is an astounding set-up—no office, only shopping, parties, hair dressers, more parties—you can cancel official programmes due to ill-health, but no social cancellations.'

It was news to me that I had been posted to London. I made discreet enquiries. The news was correct, but Mrs Pandit had rejected the proposal to have me as her private secretary. Her veto prejudiced me against her.

On 12 August 1960 I received a most extraordinary letter from Krishna Masi.

Natwar, ... my sister has played another foul trick on me and stabbed me in the back. I am coming to Delhi on the 13th evening by plane—10.30 or something with Raja [her husband] and am going to have it out once and for all with the PM ...

Love,

Masi

What was the 'stab' in the back? Krishna Masi had visited the headquarters of the famous German car manufacturer Mercedes-Benz. The establishment, aware of who she was, had gifted her a Merc. She had accepted the offer, and the car was being shipped to Bombay. Mrs Pandit informed her brother of this glaring impropriety. The matter grew into a family quarrel. The PM loathed adjudicating between his sisters. He asked Lal Bahadur Shastri to defuse this domestic crisis.

Lal Bahadurji, with his endearing capacity for elliptical, non-partisan ambiguity, brought out a solution which satisfied the elder sister without offending the younger too much—she could keep the car but should pay for it.

Both sisters were rather hot-headed, saying and doing things which in calmer moments they regretted. Krishna Masi lacked the magic which made her elder sister so formidable a social and diplomatic figure. Their rivalry made them both vulnerable and frustrated, the younger more than the elder. Both indulged in inspired indiscretion. I soon realized that their niece, Indira Gandhi, preferred *choti phuphi* to the elder one.

In September 1963 Mrs Pandit was sent as leader of the Indian delegation to the annual session of the UN General Assembly in New York (incidentally, she had been elected president of the General Assembly in 1953, the first woman to hold the post). Remembering the London posting episode

I did not look forward to her arrival. But fate plays strange tricks—benign and not so benign. I had by now got to know Mrs Pandit's youngest daughter, Rita Dar, well. Her husband was number two in our embassy in Washington. She was the most ebullient and vivacious woman I had ever met. To my horror she asked her mother that she select me as her secretary during her three-month sojourn in New York.

I had not even gone to receive her at the airport. All the other mission officers had done so.

I asked Rita how come I had been chosen to serve her mother. With a straight but slightly red face she answered, 'I haven't the foggiest idea', but assured me not to worry, 'Mummy is the nicest person in the world. You will adore her.'

The next day I presented myself at Mrs Pandit's suite in the Carlyle Hotel. She greeted me with a combination of authority and grace. 'Stop calling me madam,' she said. 'What do you call Betty [her sister]?' 'Masi,' I said. 'You can call me that too,' she replied. Rita had obviously built up a good impression of me. For a few days I resisted the masi familiarity, but not for long.

Although sixty-three years of age, she had retained her stunning looks. Not a wrinkle on her face. And what a voice—one could not resist falling for it. Unlike her sister she was a star. We soon took to each other. When John F. Kennedy died in November 1963, Mrs Pandit asked me to accompany her to the president's funeral. It was an impressively organized event. After the burial Mrs Jacqueline Kennedy held a memorial reception at the White House for the leaders who had come for the funeral from across the world. I walked in with Mrs Pandit and B.K. Nehru (then India's ambassador to the US, and Nehru's cousin), who in his memoirs has called my audacity a high-class gate crash!

12

A Tale of Three Stephanians

St Stephen's college, Delhi, has the distinction of producing two presidents, Fakhruddin Ali Ahmed (India) and Zia-ul-Haq (Pakistan). I had much to do with the latter when I was ambassador to Pakistan in the early 1980s. The St Stephen's link helped me to establish a working rapport with him. This was strictly confined to non-political, non-official matters. As I have said elsewhere, the line dividing the formal and the informal was clearly drawn by both sides.

Islamabad is among the most coveted posts in the Indian Foreign Service. It is also the most challenging, and hugely important. The Indian ambassador/high commissioner to Pakistan falls in a special category. He is under intense, round-the-clock surveillance. In Islamabad his contacts with non-establishment Pakistanis are minimal. That is not so in Lahore or Karachi, which are both lively, immensely hospitable, culturally rich, politically aggressive, stimulating, hedonistic, exuberant. Lahore is macho; Karachi is more cosmopolitan. In their different ways both are warm-hearted. Karachi because of the Muhajirs is far more welcoming to Indian diplomats and visitors. Though the architecture in Karachi is ghastly. Parts of Lahore remind one of old Delhi. Both cities consider Islamabad an upstart half-city with no proper place in history.

President Zia was a genius when it came to public relations. Even the humblest Indian was treated as a VIP and seldom denied an audience. When it came to Indo-Pak relations he was a different man. And this was the side that really mattered. He never missed an opportunity to play the Kashmir card. It was old hat and I knew how to deal with it.

In 1981 St Stephen's college was to celebrate its centenary. President Zia-ul-Haq wished to be in Delhi for the occasion. Mrs Indira Gandhi was not keen on such a visit. Not to slip on a PR opportunity, he telephoned the college principal, Rajpal, on 1 February 1981, the exact centenary date. Towards the latter half of 1980 I had requested the president to write an article for the centenary issue of the college magazine, *The Stephanian*. He had readily agreed. After several reminders he produced one which reached just in time for the deadline.

On my return to Islamabad after attending the centenary function, I presented to President Zia a copy of the *The Stephanian*, which carried his article. A few days later he sent for me. 'Natwar sahib, I want you to do me a favour.' This was most unusual. I was caught unawares and produced a nervous smile. He asked me to relax, adding, 'I am not asking for Kashmir.' He told me that he had read an article by Augustine Paul in the college magazine. (I had not read it.) Paul in his article had recalled his sharing a room with President Zia in the college hostel in the early 1940s. He had done better than the president in the Officers' Training Corps (OTC) at college and ruefully wrote: 'In spite of my above achievement in the OTC it is a typical irony of fate that it was to be Zia who later opted for the army and has risen to his present position, whereas I have to derive satisfaction from my sedentary job as an officer in the Indian Foreign Service.'

The president handed me a letter addressed to Augustine Paul. Also an autographed photo of himself. He asked me to forward these to Paul. It took me a while to locate him. He was serving as second secretary in the Indian embassy in Bangkok.

After a few weeks the president enquired if I had forwarded his letter and photograph to Paul. He had not heard from him. Fancy a busy head of state keeping track of so insignificant an epistolary exercise. I assured him that I would immediately find out why Paul had not written to thank him.

I asked Paul for an explanation. Here one sees the law of unintended consequences working with a vengeance. It was a cruel experience for the innocent Paul. As a rule-abiding foreign service officer he had informed his superiors in the embassy that he had received a letter and an autographed photograph from the president of Pakistan. The full force of the suspicious wrath of the unimaginative intelligence agencies all but pulverized Paul. How long had he been corresponding with the Pakistani president, when did he get to know him? Why should the head of an unfriendly state write to a second secretary in the Indian embassy in Thailand? It took some effort on my part to get the man off the bureaucratic noose. In those times so much suspicion infected both sides that it nearly ruined a man's career. Eventually, Paul sent a correct and respectful letter of thanks to President Zia-ul-Haq. He implored me to request President Zia to forget him and never to write to him. When I related the incident to the president of Pakistan, he was both amused and distressed.

13

The Gentleman Politician

The eighth president of the Republic of India, R. Venkataraman, served his country well and for long. A man of integrity and virtue, he did nothing indecorous or distasteful. In a polluted political environment, he brought in grace and civility, sound judgement, steady nerves and commitment. A religious south Indian Brahmin, he was a judicious secularist. He did not allow his religion to stand in the way of his official duties.

He was, after S. Radhakrishnan, the most effective vice-chairman of the Rajya Sabha. His authority was seldom, if ever, flouted. He once helped me out when I landed myself in a pickle in the Rajya Sabha.

I was elected to the Lok Sabha on 31 December 1984. Venkataraman was then vice-president. In some ways he was of the Rajaji tradition, though not as austere or as learned. south Indian Brahmin politicians generally score over their north Indian colleagues. Of course I refer to the sensible, sensitive and the sober, not those who, in the House, use their muscles, not their minds.

Venkataraman worked with four prime ministers. Some lasted a few months, others longer. He dealt with them wisely, offered advice to reduce their burden, and cleared their doubts. After the entirely unexpected assassination of Rajiv Gandhi, a great responsibility fell on him. He conducted himself with calm self-assurance and was a source of strength to the grieving family.

Having held the important finance and defence portfolios, Venkataraman was well-versed with the workings of the Central government. The obvious power centres are the prime minister and the president. It is, therefore, imperative that the two work in tandem. Pandit Nehru's relations with Dr Rajendra Prasad were not cordial. They differed on the implementation of the Hindu Code Bills; they differed on the reconstruction of the Somnath temple in Gujarat. Nehru was, on occasion, publicly impatient with the president. I remember one instance. The prime minister was leaving for Iran. Most ministers and diplomats had come to the airport to see him off. I, too, had escorted the Dalai Lama to the airport. The president had, out of politeness, decided to see off the prime minister. Nehru was getting restless, walking up and down, swagger stick in hand. He kept badgering Tandon, the chief of protocol, who told him that the president had left the Rashrapati Bhavan. After a few more minutes, the prime minister again enquired and Tandon replied, 'Sir, he is half-way.' 'Is he walking?' asked the momentarily petulant prime minister.

Nehru's relation with S. Radhakrishnan was more than close. Both being intellectuals and writers, they spoke the same language. However, Indira Gandhi had a falling out with Radhakrishnan. I was then working for her. She did not support him for a second term. Venkataraman would later play a vital role during the tenure of her son. When President Giani Zail Singh's relations with Rajiv Gandhi became more than strained, Venkataraman's decisive, wise role as mediator saved an extremely serious and ugly constitutional crisis. Only a man of his sagacity and temperament could have done so.

In his presidential memoirs, I get more than one mention. The president, being a Tamilian and a friend of Tamil Nadu chief minister M.G. Ramachandran, took a keen interest in maintaining cordial relations between India and Sri Lanka, especially following the 29 July 1987 Indo-Sri Lankan agreement.

For almost two decades, I observed Venkataramanji from close quarters and read his speeches (mostly drafted by his scholarly secretary Gopalkrishna Gandhi). I too drafted one, of which he used only half. I cannot claim intimacy with the president, however.

Like Dr Radhakrishnan, Venkataraman embodied the best in our culture and civilization: *vidya*, *tapa*, *daana*, *gyana*, *sheel*, *abhaya* and *dharma*, along with *sahitya, kala* and *sangeet.* He was exemplary.

14

Lord Mountbatten's Obsession

There was a time when I wrote lyrically and uncritically about Lord Louis Mountbatten, the man who partitioned India within three months of his arrival. Some years ago I even wrote a ten-page laudatory essay on him.

I have now become a revisionist. While not sharing Nirad C. Chaudhuri's venomous disdain for Lord Louis (see *Thy Hand, Great Anarch!*), nor the savagery of Andrew Roberts (see *Eminent Churchillians*), I have become a benign critic. His Indian record has not only to be reassessed but, more importantly, demythologized. I share the balanced but severe indictment of his lordship by George Verghese in his autobiography, *First Draft: Witness to the Making of Modern India*.

I still cherish the memory of our personal relations and have published a number of his letters to me. His genuine sympathy and condolences meant much to my wife and me, when her father, Maharaja Yadavindra Singh of Patiala, died suddenly on 17 June 1974 in the Hague. He was the Indian ambassador to Holland.

Here, I write about an incident in which the less attractive side of Mountbatten shows up.

In late 1974 it was decided that Prince Charles would stop in India for a couple of days in February 1975 on his way to Nepal for the king's coronation. His granduncle, Lord Mountbatten, was to accompany him.

At a reception at the Soviet embassy in London, Mountbatten took me aside. His grouse was that the portraits of himself and his wife had been dumped in the basement of Rashtrapati Bhavan. He reminded me that Pandit Nehru, Sardar Patel, Maulana Azad and Rajaji had all agreed that the portraits were to be displayed in the corridor connecting Ashok Hall and the grand dining room for all time. The rumour of their alleged shift grated on him. Such trivia often occupied his rover scout mind. I conveyed to him my ignorance, assuring him that I was soon leaving for India and would ascertain the facts.

I arrived in New Delhi a few days ahead of the royal duo. I informed Mrs Indira Gandhi of my encounter with Mountbatten (not one of her favourite people) who considered our alleged folly a case of lèse-majesté. She instructed me to go to Rashtrapati Bhavan and see for myself and report to her.

The not-so-celebrated portraits had indeed been shifted. Their new resting place was not the basement, however. Actually they had been installed in an even more conspicuous place than their earlier perch. They now had the company of the portraits of Jawaharlal Nehru and C. Rajagopalachari.

On a chilly 20th February morning (2.25 a.m. to be exact) I accompanied Vice-president B.D. Jatti to Palam airport to receive the heir to the British throne and Lord Louis, who on spotting me made a beeline for me and asked, 'Natwar, what about my portraits?' At 2.30 in the morning! Heaven above. I informed him that the portraits had not been relegated to the basement. He was not satisfied and asked if they were still at their original place. I told him he would be happy to know that their new location was even more prominent than the original one. He would not let go. 'So, they have been shifted.' 'Yes, they have been,' I replied. His unease was discernible.

Next morning, he went to the basement of the Rashtrapati Bhavan. I then took him to the new sanctum. He was fully satisfied. A crisis of sorts had been averted.

There was an amusing sequel. Prince Charles, though fond of his granduncle Dickie, resented his admonitions: 'Charles, put on our sweater, you will catch cold,' and that too in public.

Before taking off on the 26th for Kathmandu, the prince asked me at Palam whether he could come to India in October for a longer visit, 'but without uncle Dickie.' I replied that he would be most welcome. 'As for Uncle Dickie, your Royal Highness, that is for the House of Mountbatten-Windsor to decide.'

15

How PV Became PM

Jawaharlal Nehru and P.V. Narasimha Rao did not have much in common except that they both were intellectuals. Nehru's intellectualism was shaped by Harrow, Cambridge and Lincoln's Inn. By Bernard Shaw, Bertrand Russell, the Fabians. He probably dreamt in English. The title of his book, *The Discovery of India*, is a disarming confession of his need for discovering the land of his birth.

Rao came from a humble home. His intellectual centre was India. Unlike Nehru, his knowledge of Sanskrit was profound. His speech on Mahatma Gandhi at the UNESCO on 11 May 1995 was a masterpiece. One has only to read his address on 'India's Cultural Influence on Western Europe since the Age of Romanticism' given at Alpach, Austria, on 19 June 1983 to realize that PV was a man of learning, a scholar, a linguist and a thinker of the first order. His roots were deep in the spiritual and religious soil of India. He did not need to 'discover India'.

In early 1990 he had decided to retire from politics. He had made all arrangements to go back to Hyderabad.

He used one word where two might do. He once told me that some things should be left unsaid. He conveyed a serene calmness. At the same time he was no saint. His private life inclined towards passion and sensuality. Very few were privy to this aspect of his life. He was astute, crafty, patient. Also capable of biting sarcasm. He smiled without a smile. Nehru had a temper. PV, a temperament.

On 21 May 1991 a devastating and murderous tsunami hit Rajiv Gandhi. He was in the prime of his life. He had come to Bharatpur, my constituency, to help me in the 1991 elections, on 16 May, accompanied by his close friend Suman Dubey. A nicer and self-effacing man one could seldom find. The next day we drove to Agra. That was the last time I saw him. I wrote in an article two days later, 'The country weeps. The world mourns. I feel a terrible emptiness within and there is no drowning this sorrow. At the moment our consolations are few, our torments many. When the tears have dried, the anger subsided, the horror diminished, the scar will remain. So will the heartache.'

For his funeral many world leaders arrived in Delhi. The US vice-president Dan Quayle, Prince Charles, Yasser Arafat, Benazir Bhutto and Nawaz Sharif, the king of Bhutan, the deputy PM of the USSR, the foreign minister of China to name a few.

Before leaving Delhi most of the VIPs called on Mrs Sonia Gandhi at 10 Janpath. I was present at many of the meetings. Sonia Gandhi's world had shattered. In public she lost her composure only once. This grief was no ordinary grief. I distinctly remember the late Begum Benazir telling Sonia Gandhi and her children that after such a tragedy she should keep away from politics and look after her son and daughter. Sonia Gandhi sat in silent sorrow. Both her children said that this was not the time for such matters. Benazir again laboured the point. I then said to her that she had herself not followed what she was preaching. 'You have stepped in the shoes of your father. The Gandhis have a tradition and legacy of serving India. They cannot abandon that heritage.' Her response was that 'these were seductive words' which belied reality, etc. This was no occasion to bandy words with Begum Bhutto. The meeting ended on a sober note.

After the kings and captains departed, intense political activity was evident. The aspirants to succeed Rajiv included the late Arjun Singh, N.D. Tiwari, Sharad Pawar and Madhavrao Scindia. Sonia Gandhi was aware of this. I told her that the time had come for her to indicate her preference for the presidentship of the Congress, who would naturally become prime minister. For so momentous a decision, I suggested that she ask P.N. Haksar for advice. She said she would let me know. Meanwhile she had been consulting several other people, including M.L. Fotedar.

The next day she asked me to bring Haksar to 10 Janpath. Haksar's advice was to offer the presidentship of the Congress to Vice-president Shankar Dayal Sharma. He suggested that Aruna Asaf Ali and I should meet the vice-president. (Some overenthusiastic meddlers have created the impression that they had been asked to meet the vice-president. The most prominent among them was T.N. Kaul.) Mrs Asaf Ali said to the vice-president that she and I had been asked to see him to request him to accept the Congress party's presidentship. In other words, he would be the next prime minister. Dr

Sharma gave us a patient hearing. He then said that he was touched and honoured by Soniaji placing so much trust in him. However, what followed staggered Mrs Ali and me. The vice-president continued, 'The prime ministership of India is a full-time job. My age and health would not let me do justice to the most important office in the country. Kindly convey this to Soniaji.' His answer was wholly unexpected. To turn down the prime ministership of India was something only a man of tremendous self-confidence and integrity could do.

On the way back Arunaji and I hardly exchanged a word, because Shankar Dayal's response had overwhelmed us.

We reported to Mrs Gandhi the vice-president's decision. The country was without a prime minister. Such a hiatus could not be prolonged. Already the media was reporting unseemly and not-so-innocent jockeying for the job. Once again Sonia Gandhi turned to P.N. Haksar, who advised her to send for P.V. Narasimha Rao. The rest is history.

16

The Born Dissenter

Five non-fiction books by Indian authors (in English) will, in my judgement, still be in print fifty years from now. These are:

- *Gitanjali* by Rabindranath Tagore
- *The Story of My Experiments with Truth* by Mahatma Gandhi
- *An Idealist View of Life* by S. Radhakrishnan
- *An Autobiography* by Jawaharlal Nehru
- *The Autobiography of an Unknown Indian* by Nirad C. Chaudhuri

Today I am writing about Nirad C. Chaudhuri, who was born on 23 November 1897 and died on 1 August 1999 at the age of 101, in Oxford. Fame knocked on his door rather late in life. He was fifty-four when his *The Autobiography of an Unknown Indian* was published. The unknown Indian became known. The book is an intellectual and spiritual portrait of himself. NCC enriched the Republic of Letters.

I knew Nirad babu intimately for forty-five years. We had serious differences. His *schadenfreude* (pleasure in another's misery) was inflicted on Jawaharlal Nehru and E.M. Forster. I held both in high regard. Nirad babu was not an easy man to get on with. He was dogmatic, stubborn, self-opinionated and cantankerous. For these failings and his Anglophilism he rightly came under heavy fire. On the other hand he was a real scholar, whose erudition was wide-ranging and formidable. He wrote superb English. His style was clear, emphatic, robust, uncompromising. He was proud of his character, his integrity and his learning. He knew his worth.

If one overlooked his temperamental angularities and idiosyncrasies, one could feel his goodness and warmth. Even when our relations were under acute strain, mutual affection was not abandoned. I am writing this at a time when ethical and moral conduct is in short supply. The value system is being battered day in and day out. The squalid is edging out the sublime. Nirad Chaudhuri's life has important lessons for us. He often quoted Plato's profound maxim that 'the unexamined life is not worth living'. At another place he wrote, 'Moral discipline was an indispensable preliminary to spiritual achievement.'

In the summer of 1954 Nirad Chaudhuri wrote a scathingly critical article about Forster and his novel *A Passage to India*. It was published in the literary magazine *Encounter*, edited by the English poet Stephen Spender. I had by then got to know Forster well. I showed the article to him. He scribbled a few remarks on the margin. On my return to India, I wrote a short article on Forster in the *The*

Illustrated Weekly of India. Nirad babu read it. He referred to it when we met at dinner at St Stephen's College. Friendship followed. I was surprised when Nirad babu on the eve of his first visit to England in 1955 asked me if Forster would meet him. I wrote to Forster. He replied promptly:

> Now I get your line about Mr Chaudhuri. I had a letter about him from the British Council earlier in the day. They suggested our meeting, and I replied to them that if he cared to write to me direct, I should hope to fix something. It is up to him to write, I think, after the way he snubbed my poor Aziz (in *Encounter*).

They met in Cambridge. Forster liked Nirad babu.

In the 25 June 1998 issue of *The Illustrated Weekly of India* Nirad Chaudhuri referred to my calling him an Anglophile.

> On the whole I should be reconciled to my ill-fame. But a recent comment on me in this paper by my young friend, Kunwar Natwar Singhji, has given me the idea of delivering a sermon on the subject. He wrote: 'His reputation as an Anglophile is his doing, but he is a better Indian than most of us.' He also observed that I should continue to stir the Indian air so that he and others could breathe freely. This was very handsome of Kunwar Sahib, and I in my turn would say to him: 'To support to me is more patriotic than becoming a champion of E.M. Forster.'

I replied in the same paper, concluding sarcastically, 'It is better to be a champion of Forster than to be a cheerleader for Kipling.'

He had moved to Oxford in 1970. By the mid-1980s his readership was dwindling, so much so that he could not find a publisher for the second volume of his autobiography, *Thy Hand, Great Anarch!* Chatto & Windus, to whom NCC sent the manuscript, told him that they could not publish a 1,000-page book, so could he reduce it to 500 pages. NCC refused. Soon I heard about this troubling development. I spoke to Graham Greene, the nephew of the well-known novelist, when he came to see me in Delhi in 1986. I told him that NCC was ninety years old and a great writer. The least the publisher could do was give him a birthday present by publishing the second volume of his memoirs. Greene was a director of Chatto & Windus. He made sure that *Thy Hand, Great Anarch!* was published without cuts.

A year later, in 1987, I was one of the guest speakers at the opening session of the twenty-third International Publishers Association Congress in London. Among the speakers was Roy Jenkins, who was at the time chancellor of Oxford University. I mentioned Nirad C. Chaudhuri to him. I also suggested that Oxford should honour him in some way, like awarding him an honorary degree. Two years later, on 3 March 1990, NCC was given the honorary degree of Doctor of Letters by Oxford.

17

Fenner, JP and the Emergency

The declaration of the Emergency on 26 June 1975 produced in London a degree of disbelief combined with fiery hostility. As the weeks and months rolled on, the criticism became vicious and the hostility pernicious. *The Times*, London, carried a full-page appeal for the release of Jayaprakash Narayan. It was signed by some of the most ardent supporters and friends of India. I shall mention a few: Mrs Laski, wife of the late Harold Laski, Lady Cripps, wife of Sir Stafford, activist and politician Fenner Brockway, Dame Sybil Thorndike, journalist Anthony Howard, historian John Grigg, and several members of the British parliament, media barons and writers. It was by any measure a formidable anti-Emergency document.

Lord Mountbatten, at a reception held by Queen Elizabeth II, upbraided High Commissioner B.K. Nehru and me. 'You have locked up my friends,' said he. The friends were the Rajmatas of Gwalior and Jaipur, who were being held in

Tihar Jail. So was the erstwhile Maharaja Brigadier Bhawani Singh. Mountbatten did not speak softly; he made sure that what he said was heard by many prominent guests.

I was a regular book reviewer for the influential *New Statesman*, a weekly read by Nehru, Radhakrishan and many other Left-oriented Indian intellectuals. I was dropped from the panel of reviewers. Sanjay Gandhi was put on the cover of *The Economist*: 'The Son Also Rises' ran the heading. An agitated Dr S. Gopal, the historian, son of former president S. Radhakrishnan, came to see me. He was not given to verbal recklessness. He chose his words carefully. 'Natwar, fancy Nehru's daughter doing this,' he said to me.

A majority of the Indian community was critical. The high commission was fire-fighting on numerous fronts with little success. But the most persistent voice was that of Fenner Brockway. He was a Labour MP. He took up the case of Jayaprakash Narayan, whom he knew well. Fenner's barbs and arrows were inflicting fresh wounds by the day. His India credentials were impeccable. He had known Gandhiji and Jawaharlal Nehru. He first came to India in 1927 and had attended the Congress plenary session in Madras. His was a crusade in fortissimo. He was by no means a person who could be ignored.

I sought an appointment to present our case and JP's 'conduct' in the weeks before the declaration of the Emergency. There are times when diplomacy misfires. My mission did. When I had unloaded my sanctimonious brief, Fenner came out with all guns firing. 'Mr Deputy High Commissioner, how long have you known JP?' His tone was that of a man who was elementally indignant. I said I had met

Narayan a few times and held him in high regard. Fenner Brockway told me that he had known JP for many years.

> You people sent him to London in 1971 to talk to British parliamentarians about the situation in East Pakistan and how the government was dealing with it. I arranged a meeting in the House of Commons for him to talk to many members. He made an excellent impression. Now you tell me he is a traitor. No one believes you.

Brockway could not have put it more bluntly. I suggested to him that he write to Mrs Gandhi telling her what he had said to me. This he did. I forwarded his letter to the prime minister. Uncharacteristically, she did not respond.

I too wrote to her. 'I know what to say to our critics. I do not know what to say to our friends.' I received no reply. My own initial enthusiasm for the Emergency was misplaced—my loyalty to her precluded objectivity. I was genuinely confused. As an IFS officer it was my duty to justify the Emergency, even though aspects of it could not be explained away. My activities during that time do not rebound to my credit. I consoled myself by repeating a quotation from Goethe, 'Life isn't fun, life isn't a burden, life is a task.'

I came to Delhi for consultations in December 1975 and 1976. By and large the first six months of the Emergency had not produced outrage. When I met Indira Gandhi in 1975, she was relaxed. Nevertheless, the arrests of Jayaprakash Narayan, Morarji Desai, Atal Behari Vajpayee, Charan Singh and others could not be justified, but criticism was stifled due to rigorous press censorship. In December 1976 however a worrying sea change had occurred. I saw her but she was far from relaxed. Very deferentially I said that Sanjay was attracting widespread adverse criticism in England. This must be so in other countries as well. When I said, 'Madam, we can't pretend he does not exist,' her response was an intimidating look. Words were unnecessary. Even a mild form of lèse-majesté was not permitted. I took my leave, feeling rather miserable.

While in Delhi I heard about the darker side of the Emergency. Rigorous press censorship, forced vasectomies, the strange and severe behaviour of Sanjay Gandhi. For all practical purposes he was in charge and intolerant of people who crossed his path. It was power without responsibility. It was not a pretty picture.

On return to London I met someone at the office of Amnesty International to get a more objective view of the Emergency. It was a futile effort. I do remember him speaking at some length about George Fernandes who was apparently having a very rough time in jail.

I did however succeed in getting an invitation for Michael Foot to spend some time in India. He was at the time number two in the cabinet of Prime Minister James Callaghan. He was well received. He met Mrs Gandhi and other leaders. We also succeeded in persuading him to make a trip to Kashmir, the first and only member of the British cabinet to visit the Valley. His was a lone voice. The media did not let up. To add to our misery was the prime minister's declaration, 'The high commission was not functioning well'!

18

The Perils of Diplomacy

In November 1983, over forty heads of state and government came to Delhi for the Commonwealth summit. So did Queen Elizabeth II in her capacity as head of the Commonwealth. She does not participate in the deliberations. She meets each head of delegation and hosts a banquet for them. While the queen and her husband, Prince Philip, stayed at Rashtrapati Bhavan, the heads of delegations were put up in hotels.

The prime minister had appointed me chief coordinator. On the second day of the summit, Mrs Gandhi asked me to quietly enquire from Rashrapati Bhavan if the queen was holding an investiture for conferring the Order of Merit on Mother Teresa. Rashtrapati Bhavan confirmed what the prime minister had heard. Invitations for the investiture had been issued, that too on Buckingham Palace stationery, without consulting the secretary or the military secretary to President Giani Zail Singh.

I conveyed this to the PM, who did not like what she heard. Meanwhile, Bharatiya Lok Dal MP H.N. Bahuguna had written to the PM saying that he had from his own sources gathered that the queen was to hold an investiture at Rashtrapati Bhavan for Mother Teresa. He hoped that what he had heard was incorrect. He rightly emphasized that only the president of India could hold an investiture at Rashtrapati Bhavan. If the queen were to go ahead with her plan, then he and other Opposition leaders would be compelled to raise the matter in the Lok Sabha.

Bahuguna was right. The British, who are known for their expertise on ceremonials, had seriously erred. That error had to be rectified. It fell to my lot as chief coordinator to sort out this quite extraordinary protocol goof-up.

Mrs Gandhi asked me to get in touch with British prime minister Margaret Thatcher and report back to her. The British high commissioner, Robert Wade-Gery, was an accomplished and skilful diplomat. I asked him to convey to Mrs Thatcher and Her Majesty the Queen that the proposed investiture could not be held at Rashtrapati Bhavan. It could be held either at the UK high commission or the residence of the high commissioner. I added that we held the queen in great esteem and Mother Teresa was a very special person. But at the same time, we could not allow anything that violated a well-established Indian convention. We were surprised that we had not been consulted. Gently I reminded Wade-Gery that Her Majesty was queen of Australia, Canada and New Zealand, but not of India.

Within two hours he rang back to say that his PM felt that it was too late to change the venue. Invitations had already been sent and, above all, the queen would be inconvenienced by the change . The UK press too were aware

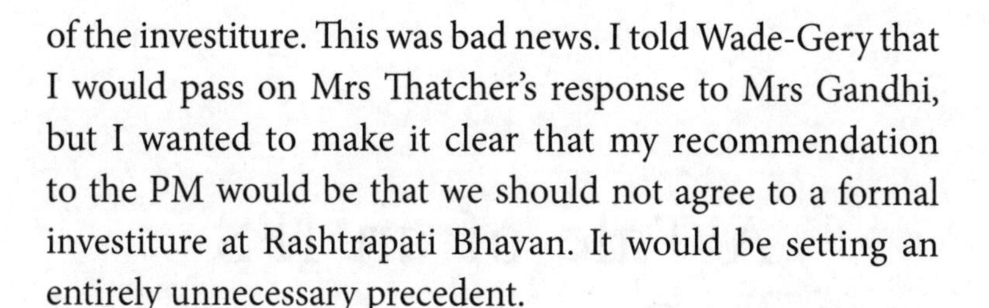

of the investiture. This was bad news. I told Wade-Gery that I would pass on Mrs Thatcher's response to Mrs Gandhi, but I wanted to make it clear that my recommendation to the PM would be that we should not agree to a formal investiture at Rashtrapati Bhavan. It would be setting an entirely unnecessary precedent.

Here was a situation that was high-grade protocol dynamite. The dramatis personae consisted of four powerful and famous ladies. Two prime ministers, one queen and the fourth, more than a saint. What if the Indian press got hold of the story? What a diplomatic bonfire they would light!

I reported to the PM what her British counterpart had said. A fleeting irritation, a moment's pause and then a masterly diplomatic googly: 'Natwar, go back to Mrs Thatcher and tell her from me that the queen can have the investiture at Rashtrapati Bhavan, but leave her in no doubt that the matter would be raised in Parliament the next day. Critical references would be made and the queen's name would be dragged in. It is only fair that the queen be made aware of this.'

No investiture was held at Rashrapati Bhavan. The queen invited Mother Teresa to tea in the Mughal Gardens where she handed her the Order of Merit. The latter remaining blissfully unaware of the upheaval she had caused. The finale was entirely satisfactory for me personally. Prime Minister Thatcher, in the concluding session of the summit, singled me out for praise. Before leaving India, the queen received me. She was gracious, and had a gift for me.

19

A Tale of an IFS Probationer

For almost thirty years after Independence, the best and the brightest young men and women opted for the IAS and the IFS. This is no longer so. The corporate sector is now attracting them. Much higher salaries is one reason; working conditions too are far superior. Globetrotting in my time was largely done by the Indian Foreign Service-wallahs. This has all changed. The IFS has lost some of its lustre.

Today I write about an unfortunate incident that occurred in our embassy in Paris in late 1959. An IFS officer who was on probation had been posted there to learn French, and was also allotted some work at the chancery. I shall call him X for reasons that shall become obvious soon. He was caught in an act of not-so-innocent theft. He panicked and tried to set fire to some official papers in the room. This misdeed was reported to the Ministry of External Affairs. The probationer was recalled to Delhi and the matter was referred to the Ministry of Home Affairs. I was at the time undersecretary there.

The home ministry with the approval of Pandit Pant, the home minister, recommended immediate dismissal of the probationer. I had no personal axe to grind. I hardly knew X. Nevertheless, I sincerely felt that dismissal was too severe a punishment. The man was in his early twenties. Dismissal would almost certainly block future employment. In true bureaucratic tradition I should not have put myself out to intercede on behalf of the offender. I was too small a fry to challenge the decision of the home minister. But I was never a pliant bureaucrat. I genuinely felt that two wrongs did not make a right. This is what I did.

Dr S. Gopal was at the time director of the historical division. He was the son of the vice-president, S. Radhakrishnan. We shared a common interest in history and literature. He was endowed with a brilliant intellect. I went to see him and narrated the melancholy tale of X to him. Also, that injustice was being done. He rightly observed that it would be difficult to put aside Pantji's decision. Did I have any alternate suggestion? I said I did. Why could the government not give X a chance to resign? Gopal was not dismissive. 'What do you want me to do?' he asked. 'Speak to your father, and request him to speak to the PM.' I was displaying outrageous cheek. Why on earth should Gopal pay any heed to me, let alone put the case before his father. To my surprise he decided to take me to the vice-president. An undersecretary wasting the time of the number two man in the country. It's not done. Fools rush in where angels fear to tread.

As ambassador to the USSR Dr Radhakrishnan had paid little heed to petty bureaucratic wooden-headedness. He heard me out. I came back confused and uncertain. Doubts assailed me. Should I have stuck my neck out this far? All I could do was wait.

Radhakrishnan, to my disbelief, did take up the case of X with Prime Minister Jawaharlal Nehru. Mercifully, he did so without mentioning my name, for frankly, I had begun to question my *auto-da-fé.* And my judgement. Had I leapt before looking? The prime minister's response, Gopal informed me, had been controlled indignation. Did the VP know that the foolish and deceitful young man had tried to set fire to the embassy, apart from stealing? The home minister had taken a decision. How could that be questioned. The vice-president said he was aware of the unacceptable conduct of the probationer who certainly deserved to be punished. But dismissal was too drastic and would almost certainly ruin his future. He suggested that the PM send for the probationer.

Two busy great men, both inspiring humanists, were concerning themselves personally with the future of an individual of little consequence. It did both much credit. So generous and considerate an approach is inconceivable in today's set-up.

I did not hear anything for the next few days. The suspense disturbed me no end. I was blaming myself for my foolhardiness. Then came relief. The prime minister's private secretary telephoned to say that the PM wished to meet X. I should bring him over. He mentioned the time and date.

I then gave X a pep talk. He was by this time enveloped in a state of acute anxiety neurosis. I told him that he was being given a chance to redeem himself. He must come clean and ask to be forgiven. I took him to the prime minister's office in South Block. X was ushered into his room. I decided not to go in and await the outcome outside. A few minutes later I was sent for. The prime minister was telling X, 'You have let me down. You will have to perform *prayaschit*.'

X was not dismissed. He was asked to resign. As I write this I ask myself: Do I have any regrets? Would I behave again today the way I did in 1959? Yes, constituted as I am, I would act as I did fifty-three years ago.

20

President Ronald Reagan Stymied

I first set foot in the White House, the official residence of the president of the United States, in November 1963. It was a sad day. The world was in mourning. The sun had set abruptly and cruelly on Camelot. Vijayalakshmi Pandit was representing India at President Kennedy's funeral in Washington. I accompanied her.

October 1987 was a happier occasion. Rajiv Gandhi, after participating in the Commonwealth summit in Vancouver, flew to Washington DC to parley with President Ronald Reagan. We were received at Andrew's airbase by Secretary of State George Shultz. The formal ceremonial reception was the next day at the White House. Reagan and Rajiv Gandhi made brief statements. These included calculated ambiguity and avoidance of any commitment. There were no new ideas. The established rules of diplomacy were observed.

Before the two delegations met at a plenary session, Rajiv Gandhi and Ronald Reagan met one on one at the Oval

Office. Sensitive issues like the Nuclear Non-Proliferation Treaty, Kashmir, the US role in Latin America were taken up.

The president, although thirty-three years senior to the prime minister, asked him to call him Ron. The PM asked the president to call him Rajiv. Mrs Indira Gandhi had been very formal in this regard. No question of her being on first names with either Reagan or Nixon. Always Mr President. They, too, stuck to Madam Prime Minister.

Ron and Rajiv got on famously. They were comfortable in each other's company. Both enjoyed irreverent jokes. Reagan was an accomplished raconteur. Their sophisticated informality broke down several barriers, without short-circuiting well-established diplomatic norms.

At the plenary session the two leaders were assisted by their principal advisers. On the American side, Vice-president George W. Bush, General Colin Powell, banker John Whitehead, Ambassador Michael Armacost, and the US Ambassador to India, John Gunther Dean. On the Indian side, apart from me were Pratap Kaul, our man in Washington, Foreign Secretary K.P.S. Menon, joint secretaries P.K. Singh and Ronen Sen, and media adviser Sharada Prasad.

The atmosphere was pleasant. No discordant note. No tension. Ronen and P.K. took notes. The Americans were less diligent. Modern technology did their work for them. The conference room was bugged and everything said was recorded, including presidential conversations.

The plenary session was followed by lunch. As we were going into the dining room, President Reagan went into a huddle with Bush Sr and Whitehead. There was nothing for the Indian side to do except wait. What had happened that was so vital that the president had to abandon his Indian guests? We didn't have to wait long. Reagan walked up to Rajiv Gandhi, apologised, then informed him that the market had crashed—the Hong Kong stock exchange had stopped transactions. Reagan was asked whether Wall Street would follow suit. For the time being he had decided against it and would wait and see. Bush Sr asked Rajiv Gandhi to be excused for a few minutes to speak to the treasury secretary.

It must be said for President Reagan that not for a moment did he appear worried or preoccupied during the lunch. His composure was impressive. Bush Sr rejoined us. All was almost well. Whitehead then left. He was more suited to finance than to foreign affairs (he had been a stockbroker) and was the right person to keep track of the financial earthquake.

The menu was not ducal, but neither was it austere. Wines, red or white, were forbidden for the Indian side. The pantry was close by and it comforted me no end to hear the din emanating from that quarter. It felt like home.

Despite Wall Street, the mood at lunch was relaxed, even jovial. The president was in good form. We were aware of his impressive stock of amusing anecdotes and jokes. He told them with an actor's verbal skill. Anyone with a sense of humour delighted Rajiv Gandhi.

After the first course President Reagan was in his element. His jokes about Gorbachev and Thatcher were out of the top drawer. It was obvious that he was himself the author of these amusing nuggets. Rajiv Gandhi nudged me. I produced one. It was mildly naughty. K.P.S. Menon, Jr also contributed another. Score: two all. Mr Reagan then changed gear.

He said to Rajiv Gandhi that earlier in the week he had met a remarkable and courageous Chinese lady. She had suffered and survived the Cultural Revolution in China. Her daughter had been driven to her death. This lady was now living in Washington. She had written a book about her hair-raising experiences. Reagan then paused. That gave me an opening. I said, 'Mr President, the lady's name, if I am not mistaken, is Nien Cheng. Her book *Life and Death in Shanghai* is a deeply moving account and indictment of the Cultural Revolution. It is a triumph of the human spirit.' The president hadn't expected this. K.P.S. Menon referred to the lady as having appeared at the Indian consulate in Shanghai. This was one of the crimes she was accused of. She had written about it in her book. Our American friends began to look at us rather incredulously. Next P.K. Singh also pointed to another incident in the book. Three out of six members of the Rajiv Gandhi team had read the book. Not one among the Americans!

President Reagan thereafter left the topic of Mrs Chang. He pulled out a notebook from his pocket and sprang a surprise on us. His friends in California had asked him to inquire from Mr Gandhi why India was not buying Californian almonds anymore? This stumped us. None of us knew. One for the Americans.

After the lunch Ambassador John Gunther Dean caught me by the elbow. 'How the hell did you guys know the president was going to speak about that ... Chinese female?' Smugly, I replied, 'John, as good diplomats we had come prepared for all eventualities, except Californian almonds.'

21

Gandhi and the Eiffel Tower

Earnest Hemingway spent his early youth in Paris in the 1920s. He fell in love with the city and wrote lyrically about it: 'If you are lucky enough to have lived in Paris as a young man, then wherever you go for the rest of your life, it stays with you, for Paris is a moveable feast.'

My first glimpse of Paris was in the autumn of 1952. It has stayed in my imagination ever since. André Malraux, the cultural tsar in Charles de Gaulle's government, made the city sparkle by giving it a good scrubbing. French history, culture and literature became part of my consciousness and sharpened my aesthetic sensitivity. It was a deliberate attempt on my part to distance myself from the overwhelming English (rather than British) influence on my intellectual development. I did not even partially succeed. As far as Paris and France are concerned, I have retained my wholesale admiration, which sometimes degenerates into dilettantism.

Travelling with Indira Gandhi and Rajiv Gandhi was a treat. Travelling with Prime Minister Manmohan Singh was altogether a different experience. Foreign ministers should, as far as possible, avoid accompanying prime ministers on their foreign visits. The focus, rightly, is on the PM. Foreign ministers have little to do, except to camouflage their redundancy. At best the advantages of such a visit could be that one gets a grandstand view of how the world and its nations are run. It is, broadly speaking, a disillusioning experience. The heads of governments are rushing from one appointment to another. They produce phoney smiles and shake the hands of foreign ministers while looking over their heads. A handful does offer sparks of an inspiring vision. I often wonder how such mediocre individuals make it to the top. I, of course, never for one moment underestimate the potency of mediocrity. How very right was the famous Swedish aristocrat, Count Axel Oxenstierna, who said, 'Know my son, with how little wisdom the world is governed.' Luck, undeniably, is a major player—in other words, a good horoscope can do wonders, as so memorably highlighted by Dr Homi Bhabha, our greatest physicist. Jawaharlal Nehru once teasingly said to Bhabha, 'Homi, how can *you* of all people dabble in this nonsense about horoscopes? I take it the rumour is unfounded'. Homi's answer, 'Sir, the rumour is well founded. I have often posed the question to myself: "How could Panditji include such C category individuals in his cabinet?" The answer is that the ministers have powerful horoscopes.' Nehru smiled and changed the subject.

On 9 December 1970 Charles de Gaulle died. Prime Minister Indira Gandhi immediately decided to leave for Paris to pay homage to a man for whom she had had high regard. She asked me to accompany her. No one else except one security officer. She stayed with Ambassador D.N. Chatterjee. I with Ashok Gokhle, number two in our Paris embassy. A memorial mass was held at Notre Dame cathedral. World leaders had all rushed to the French capital to pay their respects to the greatest Frenchman of the twentieth century. The occasion combined serenity with sensitivity, sobriety with style.

In the evening President Georges Pompidou gave a reception at the Élysée Palace, the official residence of the president of France. It does not have the splendour of Versailles but its interior has its own grandeur. My second pilgrimage to the Élysée was in January 1989. President François Mitterrand invited leaders of the delegation to the conference on the abolition of chemical weapons. Iran and Iraq were at war. It fell to me to keep the peace at the Élysée by placing myself between the foreign ministers of the two countries with their consent.

In early 2005, I was in Paris with Prime Minister Manmohan Singh. President Chirac invited him and me for a private dinner at the Élysée. The PM sat opposite President Chirac. I sat on his right. Since it was not a formal dinner I took the liberty of asking President Chirac if he knew what Mahatma Gandhi had written about the Eiffel Tower. A surprised Chirac confessed he had no idea about the Mahatma's views on the tower. 'Mr President, I have brought with me an extract from the Mahatma's autobiography, *The Story of my Experiments with Truth*. I gave him the sheet of paper. He kept it carefully in his pocket, after thanking me for enlightening him.

Gandhiji had, while a student in London, visited Paris in 1890 to see the great Paris exhibition. Here is what he wrote:

> I remember nothing of the Exhibition except its magnificent variety. I have a fair recollection of the Eiffel Tower, as I ascended it thrice. There was a restaurant on the first platform and just for the satisfaction of being able to say that I had had my lunch at a great height, I threw away seven shillings on it.

The Mahatma than expressed his assessment of the tower. He did not mince words. He also invoked Tolstoy and his comments on the steel contraption:

> I must say a word about the Eiffel Tower. I do not know what purpose it serves today [1927]. I then heard it greatly disparaged as well as praised. I remember that Tolstoy was the chief among those who disparaged it. He said the Eiffel Tower was a monument to man's folly, not his wisdom …

Count Leo Tolstoy, one of the greatest novelists and an acknowledged guru of the young Mohandas Karamchand Gandhi, did from time to time make quirky pronouncements.

22

A White House Invitation That Never Was

The charter of the United Nations is not an inspiring document. The only exceptions are three sentences in the Preamble. These resonate. That's about it.

> WE THE PEOPLES OF THE UNITED NATIONS DETERMINED
> to save succeeding generations from the scourge of war, which twice in our lifetime has brought untold sorrow to mankind, and
> to reaffirm faith in fundamental human rights, in the dignity and worth of the human person, in the equal rights of men and women and of nations large and small …
> AND FOR THESE ENDS
> to practice tolerance and live together in peace with one another as good neighbours …

The charter was signed on 26 June 1945, in San Francisco, at the conclusion of the United Nations Conference on International Organization, and came into force on 24 October 1945.

The UN was an act of conscience. The Americans had their own view. Even before the ink was dry, the US made sure that the UN Security Council would be an undemocratic body.

Cordell Hull, the US secretary of state, arrogantly asserted that 'the veto provision was an absolute condition for US participation in the United Nations. The superpowers would not be subject to any collective coercion. The veto ensured that the General Assembly or the Security Council could not act against the permanent five.'

In other words, the vital national interests of the P5 could not and would not be subject to scrutiny in the General Assembly or the Security Council. No wonder the Mexican delegate at San Francisco said in October 1945 that under the UN Charter 'the mice would be disciplined but the lions would be free.'

India became a founding member of the UN by virtue of her having been a member of the League of Nations. Although India was a part of the British Empire, Britain made her a member. No one objected. Indian delegates were on a short leash and were chosen carefully. Each one was an empire loyalist. Exceptions there were, but those could only speak on matters relating to health, labour or child welfare. Some of these 'safe' Indians were colourful personalities like the maharajas of Bikaner and Patiala and Aga Khan. Occasionally, the calm waters of Lake Geneva were stirred. At the best of times the League of Nations was an eviscerated organization. It was dominated by half-a-dozen European countries. The US was not yet a global power.

It was hoped that the UN would set the agenda of humankind. Alas! This did not happen. Regardless,

Jawaharlal Nehru had faith in the UN. That is why he took the Kashmir issue to the UN Security Council on 1 January 1948. A case of political innocence. In the Council the dice was loaded against India from the start.

Indira Gandhi did not look at the UN with starry eyes. She addressed the General Assembly on several occasions. In 1968 and 1970 I accompanied her. She was a star attraction and was looked up to as a leader of a great democracy and as a stateswoman representing the voice of hundreds of millions around the globe. She was a leader, not a pleader.

Her speech of 1968 was appreciated and remembered. She had ended her address with these lines from the tenth book of the Rig Veda:

> Common be your prayer;
> Common be your end;
> Common be your purpose;
> Common be your deliberation;
> Common be your desire;
> Unified be your hearts;
> United be your intentions;
> Perfect be the union amongst you.

In 1970 the UN observed its twentieth-fifth anniversary. Many world leaders came to New York for the occasion. This time Indira Gandhi's theme was a sombre appraisal of the UN's functioning during the past two-and-half decades.

Twenty-five years later, the principle of the universality of the United Nations membership does not yet prevail. The system of unilateral action and exclusive alliances has not been disowned (a subtle reference to US intervention in Vietnam). Spheres of influence and balance of power continue to actuate the policies of many nations, even though they fail to produce the desired results.

Our ambassador to the US was L.K. Jha, well known for his American tilt. Subtlety of mind was not accompanied by openness of character. A product of the Indian Civil Service, he had no strong political convictions.

Two days before the prime minister's departure from New York, Jha asked her if she would like to attend the dinner President Nixon was hosting for leaders of the delegation at the White House. She said she had received no invitation. The ambassador's reply was disingenuous. No invitations had been sent by President Nixon. It was for respective heads of mission to inform their president or prime minister of the dinner. The prime minister found this novel way of inviting heads of governments unacceptable. She rightly felt this to be a summons, not an invitation. That L.K. Jha should even have imagined that this verbal invite would be entertained appalled her. He pleaded. She asked him to convey to the White House of her inability to attend the Nixon dinner, as she had to leave New York urgently.

The ambassador next requested the PM to write to President Nixon explaining her inability to attend. Mrs Gandhi turned to me: 'Natwar, draft one.' I did. She signed it. I took it to the ambassador. He did not like what he read. 'Natwar, it is so dry. Can't you produce a less chilling letter?' 'Jha sahib, I should tell you that she will not change her mind. If I were to convey to her that you wanted an effusive one she would not even send this one.' She knew what she was doing. She took unkindly to the prime minister of India being taken for granted. What a contrast to 'Mr President [Bush], the people of India dearly love you'—a statement which Manmohan Singh will never live down. Indira Gandhi could be forgiving and charmingly gentle, but no one could be allowed to treat her in an off-hand manner. Behind the velvet glove there was steel. She made us all feel proud.

23

Castro and the New Afghan Government

Fidel Castro is unlikely to remember and I am unlikely to forget my several meetings with him. Fidel (every Cuban uses his first name)—to resort to a worn-out cliché—is a living legend. The other two are the ninety-two-year-old Nelson Mandela and the hundred-year-old General Vo Nguyen Giap who drove the French out of Vietnam fifty-five years ago.

In late 1982 I visited Havana to chalk out a strategy on how to make a NAM summit successful. The sixth summit was held in Havana in 1979 when Fidel Castro was elected chairman of the movement. The flight to Havana was an exciting ordeal: Delhi–New York–Mexico City–Havana. To me Fidel Castro is an icon. At the age of thirty-four he had ousted the US-backed dictator Fulgencio Batista—the day was 1 January 1959. That day Cuba ceased to be an American 'colony'.

An abortive coup in 1953 had landed Castro in jail. At his trial he made a memorable speech: 'I know the regime will try to suppress the truth by all possible means; I know there will be a conspiracy to bury me in oblivion. But my voice will not be stifled; it will rise from my breast even when I feel most alone, and my heart will give it all the fire that callous cowards deny it … Condemn me. It does not matter. History will absolve me.'

I had not requested a meeting with President Castro. Imagine, therefore, when on the final day of my stay, a wholly unexpected summons came from the president's office. Just four words: 'Fidel will receive you.' I was at once apprehensive and elated. The uppermost thought in my mind was: 'What do I say to him?' I need not have worried. He put me at ease right away by asking, 'Who are the Gurkhas, and what were they doing in the Falkland Islands?' I gave the Cuban leader a thumbnail history of the Gurkhas. They were ferocious warriors; their valour was legendary; most of them came from Nepal. They had served in the British Indian army; even today there was a Gurkha regiment in the British Army, which had fought in the recently concluded Anglo-Argentine war. I then asked, 'Excellency, your query about the Gurkhas surprises me.' Castro said he had come across them in Maurice Herzog's book *Annapurna*, which he had recently read. We then briefly touched on the forthcoming NAM summit in New Delhi.

On two other occasions I was given the opportunity to spend some time with the great man. At one of these meetings I asked him, 'When did you first meet Jawaharlal Nehru?' What he related was fascinating.

In September 1960, the UN General Assembly observed the fifteenth anniversary of the founding of the organization.

Many world leaders came to New York. Among the more prominent were Jawaharlal Nehru, Nikita Khrushchev, Marshal Tito, Gamal Nasser, Ahmad Soekarno, Kwame Nkrumah, Harold Macmillan, Dwight D. Eisenhower and Fidel Castro.

On arrival in New York, Castro, to his dismay and disgust, found that no hotel would put him up. Temporarily, he moved into the tiny Cuban mission to the UN. Next day, he called on the secretary general of the UN, Dag Hammarskjöld, to tell him that it was the secretary general's duty to find a place where the Cuban leader and his delegation could stay. Failing that he would pitch a tent in the UN compound and move there. Even for so unflappable a character as Hammarskjöld, this was an entirely novel approach by the leader of a member state.

Having shaken up the UN establishment, Castro moved into a hotel in Harlem in New York City. This was unprecedented. It made headlines. Castro said to me, 'Do you know which leader was the first to come to meet me in Harlem? The great Jawaharlal Nehru. I was thirty-four years of age. I was inexperienced. I was tense. I had never been to any international conference. Nehru boosted my morale, enhanced my self-confidence. I will never forget Nehru's magnanimous gesture.'

At yet another meet he let go at the USSR. 'I had been elected chairman of the NAM in September 1979. The USSR invaded Afghanistan in December, thus inflicting a near mortal blow to my chairmanship. Here I was, a friend of the USSR, and they did not even have the courtesy to take me into confidence.' Then came a Castro broadside: 'Not only that, they sent a government to Kabul in a suitcase.' This was a reference to Babrak Karmal being sent from Moscow to become president of Afghanistan. I much enjoyed his candour.

The last time I met him was in September 1988 in Havana along with Prime Minister Rajiv Gandhi. The meeting lasted six hours. Castro placed before us his *weltanschauung* (world-view) in soaring language and passion that made a lasting impression on Rajiv. It was a stunning tuition on the most intractable international issues. Granted it was a one-sided view, but Castro made a convincing case for it.

He and Rajiv Gandhi 'connected', regardless of the eighteen-year difference in their age. Both men of vision, imagination and honour.

One contrast was glaring. The Indian PM always dressed immaculately. The Cuban leader makes no concessions to sartorial elegance.

Fidel Castro is now eighty-six years. He is in semi-retirement. He makes pronouncements from time to time. The world listens. He has outlived nine US presidents and ten Indian prime ministers. A record. When he finally departs there will be a lonesome place on the horizon.

24
Cambodia and Its King

Hindu religion and culture made peaceful inroads into what till the last quarter of the twentieth century was known as Indo-China. Here two great civilizations met and coexisted. The Khmer Empire (Cambodia) was the largest and the most prosperous and sophisticated region in Southeast Asia. Even today, from Burma to Indonesia, one can witness architectural wonders which distinctly carry the stamp of Hinduism and Buddhism. Angkor Wat in Cambodia and Borobudur in Indonesia are sublime works of art. The Kambojas built a vast empire. Their rulers, called devarajas and buddharajas, ruled from Angkor. Their rule lasted from AD 150 to AD 1471.

Angkor then disappeared for nearly five hundred years under trees and forests. As happened to Ajanta and Ellora. The former was 'discovered' by a Frenchman, and the latter by an Englishman. The kingdom of Cambodia became a French colony in 1883, and remained so till the end of 1953. Between 1941 and 1945, Cambodia was in Japanese hands. Nevertheless, they allowed the French administration to continue.

The most famous and long-lasting leader of Cambodia was King Norodom Sihanouk. Jawaharlal Nehru broke journey in Phnom Penh on his way back from China in October 1954. He spent twenty-four hours there and met the young king and liked him. It was at this meeting that Sihanouk expressed his wish to attend the Bandung conference which was to be held in April 1955. Nehru told him that he looked forward to meeting him there.

Before going to Bandung, the Cambodian leader came to India for an eight-day visit—16–24 March 1955. I was appointed the liaison officer. The prime minister went to Palam airport to receive Sihanouk. Soon a plane was seen approaching the airstrip. Suddenly it pulled up. It made several rounds over the airport, the exercise lasting more than ten minutes. The PM was getting restless. No one could enlighten him on the strange antics of the pilot. Finally, it landed. Norodom Sihanouk descended from the plane in a white closed-collar coat and a black dhoti—the formal dress of his country. The PM asked him why his plane kept circling over the airport for so long. The prince told Pandit Nehru that his pilot was a French national. The aviation map he was using for his flight path only showed Safdarjung airport. We discovered that the map was published in 1936. Palam airport did not exist then. Our Cambodian friends were twenty-nine years behind time!

Even a more hilarious situation followed. The prince had brought four or five Buddhist monks with him. On the PM's instructions, we too brought our monks. Pali was their common language. Normally monks are composed and serene. However, the PM noticed that our monks appeared in a state of shock. He asked what the matter was. The reply this time was indeed unsettling. Our monks had asked the Cambodian monks what their dietary preferences were. The answer was 'beef'.

That was my first introduction to Cambodia and its king. I accompanied him to Sanchi and Bodh Gaya. After that I did not meet him for the next thirty-five years.

The Indo-China situation had become complex during the Vietnam War (1955–75). The Americans bombed Cambodia time and time again. Nixon and Kissinger played with the lives of thousands of Cambodians. One has only to read Barbara Tuchman's essay on Kissinger in her book *Practicing History* to understand that the US role in Indo-China did that country no credit. The appalling details of their activities are chronicled also in Norodom Sihanouk's *My War with the CIA*.

My sustained involvement with Cambodia began in January 1987 when I was on a visit to Hanoi. The accomplished and astute foreign minister, Nguyen Co Thach, took me aside. Hanoi had decided to pull out its troops from Cambodia by 1989. Could India convey this to the ASEAN countries? I naturally asked, 'Why India.' His answer was gratifying. 'Because you have credibility.' For Vietnam this was a geopolitical question of the highest importance.

I reported my conversation with Co Thatch to Prime Minister Rajiv Gandhi, who at once saw the significance of this Vietnamese request. He asked me to visit all the ASEAN capitals. In Singapore, Kuala Lumpur, Manila and Bangkok

I got a cold shoulder except in Phnom Penh, the capital of Cambodia. These countries did not trust Vietnam, nor believed that its offer to withdraw troops from Cambodia was genuine.

Phnom Penh was then the most dismal place I had ever visited. It did not even have a daily newspaper. Hun Sen, the prospective prime minister, enquired if India could arrange a meeting between him and King Sihanouk.

This we agreed to do. I met the deposed king in Jakarta, New York and Paris. Our efforts bore fruit. The meeting between Hun Sen and the king took place in Paris in December 1987. An agreement was reached after four rounds of meetings. The International Conference on Cambodia was held in Paris in August and September 1989. The foreign ministers of the USSR, China and France, and the US secretary of state attended. I represented India. At the conference several powerful countries were reluctant to attribute 'genocide' to the Pol Pot regime. In my statement, however, I made it clear that the Pol Pot regime (or the Khmer Rouge) was guilty of genocide in Cambodia between 1975 and 1978. The majority were of the same view.

Vietnam withdrew its troops. The process of reconciliation and reconstruction commenced (Pol Pot had killed two million Cambodians out of a population of eight million), and Cambodia gradually emerged from the menacing and murderous tunnel into light and liberty.

25

General Vo Nguyen Giap

A Master Militarist

To be a hero one must live in heroic times. General Vo Nguyen Giap is a genuine hero. His military strategy and genius for guerrilla warfare bestowed on him legendary status. I met him a number of times in Hanoi, Delhi and Kolkata.

My first meeting was in Hanoi in 1984. Before elaborating on my encounters with the diminutive general (5'2"), let me draw the attention of the reader to the character of the Vietnamese people.

The long-serving prime minister of Vietnam, Pham Van Dong, wrote:

> There is nothing else in our history except struggle. Struggle against foreign invaders, always more powerful than ourselves, struggle against nature. Because we have nowhere else to go, we have had to fight things out where we were. After two thousand years of this, our people have

> developed a very stable nervous system. *We never panic.* When a situation arises, our people say, 'Ah well, there it goes again'.

General Giap earned immortality when in May 1954 he defeated a large and well-equipped French army (which had air support) at a little-known town in north-west Vietnam. The battle of Dien Bien Phu is one of the defining moments of the twentieth century. It signalled the end of the French Empire in Indo-China. There Giap followed Mao Zedong's guerrilla war strategy: 'When the enemy advances, withdraw; when he stops, harass; when he tires, strike; when he retreats, pursue.'

The siege of Dien Bien Phu lasted fifty-five days. Giap surprised the French when he took his heavy armour to the ramparts of the French fortress, in the middle of the night, noiselessly. The French eventually surrendered. Winning the battle was step number one. The management of post-battle events was equally important. Giap said to me, 'We lost not a day in establishing an administration that ensured order, economic planning, relief and rehabilitation. We would have failed if we had not planned all this before the battle began. Finally, our ideology triumphed.'

He gave the analogy of the four wheels of a motor car. If one wheel was missing, the car could not move. Hence he ensured that ideology, military action, administrative policy and economic planning—all four worked in tandem. Success followed. On my return to Delhi, I sent Mrs Indira Gandhi a note regarding my powwow with General Giap.

Giap's intelligence services were far superior to those of the French, who relied on unreliable informers. Several times the general emphasized that he was only an instrument—the real victors were the people and the party. I did not swallow this ideological pill. For I have always held that the role of the individual—politician, soldier, reformer, or any other leader—is of supreme importance. Napoleon once famously boasted: 'Circumstances! I create circumstances.' General Vo Nguyen Giap created circumstances. He did so without boasting.

His role in fighting against the US during the Vietnam War is also a part of history. In this case, however, the glory and triumph were shared by one or two other commanders.

Giap's nationwide adulation and popularity caused unease to the party high command. Unlike the Soviets and the Chinese Communist Party, the Vietnamese Communist Party under the adorable Uncle Ho (or Ho Chi Minh) discouraged the 'cult of personality'. For a while Giap lost his seat in the politburo and was seldom mentioned by the media. After a while he re-emerged.

In 1989 General Giap came to Delhi semi-incognito. He stayed at the Ashok Hotel. I called on him. He was wearing a khaki shirt and matching trousers. After the preliminaries, he asked, 'How are things in your country?' Smugly I replied, 'General, things are going well. The Congress party has 413 members in the lower House of Parliament. Prime Minister Rajiv Gandhi's visit to China has been a great success ...' General Giap listened. What he next said I have not forgotten. 'Be careful when things go well. Don't lower your guard. Things start going wrong when they appear to be going well.' Sage advice that we did not follow. In the 1989 general elections the Congress came down to 195 MPs from 413. We had become complacent and paid a heavy price.

I last met General Giap at his home in Hanoi in 2005. My wife also accompanied me. The general was in full military regalia, 'in honour of the Indian foreign minister'. His wife played host. He spoke little. He presented us signed copies of his books and insisted on a formal 'photo opportunity'. He was then ninety-five years old. Last year he crossed hundred.

I acquired wisdom late in life. Some of it I acquired from General Vo Nguyen Giap.

26

Hastings Banda and Diplomatic Protocol

The first generation of African leaders was inspired by the Indian freedom movement: Kwame Nkrumah of Ghana (formerly Gold Coast), Jomo Kenyatta of Kenya, Kenneth Kaunda of Zambia (formerly Northern Rhodesia), Julius Nyerere of Tanzania (formerly Tanganyika), Milton Obote of Uganda, Seretse Khama of Botswana (formerly Bechuanaland) and Hastings Banda of Malawi (formerly Nyasaland).

Of these Dr Banda was the odd man out. He was a sinister and quirky dictator. Born in 1898 he spent forty-two years abroad, mostly in the UK as a practising doctor. He was intensely conservative and an opinionated elder of the Church of Scotland. His proximity to divinity was spurious. He was sixty years of age when he returned to his homeland. He converted the Nyasaland African National Congress into a mass movement. 'Very soon I hope to have the whole of Nyasaland on fire,' said the man wearing a three-piece suit, with a black homburg atop his head.

The British handling of the volatile situation was inept. The colonial office in London gave the impression of an empire on the run. Dr Banda was arrested by Governor Robert Armitage, who declared an emergency. The territory saw outbursts of violence. Banda emerged a hero. Commenting on his year-long imprisonment he said, 'It was the best turn the British ever did to me.' He was released. Nyasaland attained freedom.

Banda ruled Malawi for the next thirty years with an iron hand. His dictatorship soon became a tyranny. He appointed himself president for life in 1971. Dissent was snuffed out with brutal force. Thousands of Malawians were put in prison, where they were treated like animals. No freedom of speech. No freedom of press. No redress. No appeal. The secret police dealt with opponents with dedicated ruthlessness. In 1981 Orton Chirwa, in exile in Zambia, was abducted along with his wife, Vera Chirwa. He had studied in St Stephen's College. We met in Lusaka during my two-and-a-half-year tenure there. He related horror tales. On reaching the capital Blantyre he was charged with treason, 'tried' and condemned to death. The death sentence was then converted to life imprisonment. Two years later, three cabinet ministers were bludgeoned to death. Banda enriched himself, controlling a huge business empire.

I have given this lengthy introduction because Banda is not well known. History has passed him with an indifferent shrug.

Now comes his brief appearance in New Delhi. In November 1983 the Commonwealth summit was held in the Indian capital. Indira Gandhi was host and chairperson. I was appointed chief coordinator. The Commonwealth Heads of Government Meeting (CHOGM) is a much smaller undertaking compared to the NAM summits. Queen Elizabeth II was in Delhi to inaugurate the event. Most Commonwealth heads attended, including Dr Banda.

Mrs Gandhi hosted several dinners for the heads at the Ashok Hotel. The Malawi president handed us an unprecedented protocol tsunami. Dr Banda was a bachelor. His constant companion, for almost thirty years, had been Cecilia Kadzamira. He had employed her as a nurse in his London surgery. She returned to Malawi with him. From nurse she was promoted to become His Excellency's secretary. Her rise was rapid. In no time Madam Cecilia was appointed official hostess, eventually to become 'Mama'—mother of the nation.

She had accompanied Hastings Banda to the Delhi summit. When it came to sending an invitation to him, the question arose: to invite Mama to dinner or not.

I placed the problem before the prime minister. Open-minded and tolerant she was. But a puritan when it came to mistresses camouflaged as hostesses. No invitation for Mama Cecilia. I was perhaps the only civil servant who on rare occasions stood his ground. I told the PM that Banda would boycott the dinner if Mama was not invited. That would be noticed; the consequences could be entirely disagreeable. R.K. Dhawan, her personal secretary, supported me. After a pause Mrs Gandhi asked me, 'Does the queen invite her? Find out.' Eventually we got the answer. Her Majesty apparently had no such inhibitions. The unalluring Mama Cecilia Kadzamira was invited to Mrs Gandhi's dinner. She came. She saw. She did not conquer.

Dr Banda ruled for another decade. He lost the 1994 presidential elections. An inquiry commission found him guilty of the murder of former cabinet colleagues. He was nearly ninety-five. He was acquitted of the charges in 1996 due to lack of evidence. He shifted to Johannesburg and died in 1997 aged ninety-nine. Mama was at his bedside.

27

High-level Municipal Diplomacy

After serving five years in the prime minister's secretariat, I was appointed ambassador to Poland in May 1971. I was forty years of age, with eighteen years of service behind me. In the context of those times, it was not an insignificant post. Poland was the largest communist state in eastern Europe, and headquarters of the Warsaw Pact (an inadequate response to the NATO). Poland, along with India and Canada, was a member of the Indo-China Commission. Ninety-five per cent Poles were Catholics. It is not necessary to recall the percentage of communists. It was negligible.

Destiny inflicted a cruel geography and a tragic history on Poland. The Polish leader Wladyslaw Gomulka used to say, 'I would sacrifice a quarter of Poland for a better geography.' There was however no getting away from Germany in the west or Russia in the east. As for history, Poland was divided and partitioned more than once, and for more than a century disappeared from the map of Europe. It was the Catholic church which preserved Polish culture and language.

World War II began on 1 September 1939 when Hitler invaded and conquered Poland. Millions of Polish Jews ended up in the gas chambers of Auschwitz. Immediately after presenting my credentials I went to Auschwitz to lay a wreath and pay homage.

The capital Warsaw was mostly destroyed by the Germans. It was rebuilt brick by brick after the war. The old city courtyard is one of the great architectural sights of Europe. Nothing remained of it in 1945. It was meticulously restored by consulting old records and maps.

Indo-Polish relations were cordial and unbroken. I had easy access to the top leadership. My having accompanied Mrs Indira Gandhi on her state visit to Poland in 1967 no doubt helped. Soon after my arrival in Warsaw, my wife was struck by cerebral meningitis. Not knowing the language did not help. But for the very best medical help promptly provided by the government, my wife would not have recovered without any permanent damage. It was not an auspicious start.

However, the longer we stayed the more at home we felt. The Poles are a warm people. They loathed the USSR and were not afraid to express their views after heavy gulps of vodka.

In a little while after my arrival, I discovered that the Warsaw city authorities had named roads after Mahatma Gandhi and Jawaharlal Nehru. Rabindranath Tagore was well known and widely read. R.K. Narayan too. On 19 February 1973 fell the five hundredth birth anniversary of the most famous Polish astronomer, Nicolaus Copernicus.

He is known for the Copernican theory of the heavens. His treatise, 'De Revolutionibus Orbium Coelestium Libri' (On the Revolutions of the Celestial Spheres), earned him immortality. The timid and cautious canon (that he was), Copernicus did not dare publish the treatise for fear of Rome. The first completed copy was placed on his bed when he was nearing death in 1543.

I am no astronomer or scientist, but as an interested layman I read a bit about Copernicus. He challenged the Ptolemaic system of the universe which was the dominant thinking of his day and which asserted that the earth was at the centre of the universe with the sun, moon, planets and stars revolving around it. Heresy, punishable by imprisonment if not death. He put down seven original axioms to make his case. I shall paraphrase only three. 1. The earth is not the centre of the universe. 2. The sun is the centre of the planetary system. 3. The earth revolves round the sun.

Thus equipped I went to Torun, the city of his birth. It is a placid and beautiful place touched by the river Vistula. Next, I wrote to the Ministry of External Affairs suggesting that, to mark the five hundredth birth anniversary of Copernicus, a road in New Delhi be named after him. I thought it was an imaginative and reasonable proposal. I should have known better. After several weeks, the response came. It was disappointingly negative, delivered in impeccable bureaucratic jargon. It went something like this: 'These matters are not in the jurisdiction of the Ministry of External Affairs. The renaming of roads is not a simple exercise, etc.' Hence it was not possible for the ministry to accept my proposal. There was also a touch of asperity.

I knew how Indira Gandhi's mind worked on such matters. Routine responses she abhorred. So I wrote her a personal letter, telling her that the ministry had, in a routine way, dismissed my suggestion to name a road after Copernicus. Many roads in New Delhi were named after third-rate British viceroys and barbaric despots like Aurangzeb. The Poles had been gracious to name two roads in their capital after two great Indians. If I remember correctly, I even gave the name of the road which might be called Copernicus Marg. It was Lytton Road, where once stood Jind House. For quite some time I heard nothing till H.Y. Sharada Prasad, media adviser to the PM, informed me that Copernicus had scored over Lytton.

28

His Imperial Majesty and His Quadrupeds

During my eight decades I met a great variety of famous, fastidious and fatuous individuals. It always surprised me how some of these specimens could have become heads of state or heads of government. On their whims and vagaries depended the fate of millions.

The malevolence of some made one question whether the almighty is a democrat or a dictator. I do often wonder why the sinners outnumber the saints on a ratio of ten to one. Human motivation is not easy to fathom. Some inspire trust; others disdain. Maniacs and mahatmas coexist with unease. I have known several who have jaywalked through life; others who have lived on the edge.

A diplomat gets a grandstand view of the actions of the messy and the mighty. For example, a posting to Uganda in the 1970s could be more hazardous than exciting. One day the Uganda dictator Idi Amin sent for his foreign minister. He told him that by next week Uganda's name was to be changed to Idi. He should inform the UN and all other international organizations, airlines, etc. A week passed. Amin summoned the foreign minister. 'Did you carry out my orders?' thundered the unpredictable president. The shivering minister said that he had run into a serious problem. 'What problem?' the president enquired. 'Your Excellency, there is a country called Cyprus. The people are called Cypriots. If Uganda were to be called Idi, we would be called Idiots.'

I never met Idi Amin. I did meet several other African leaders. One or two I got to know well. The most extraordinary was His Imperial Majesty Haile Selassie I, 'Elect of God', 'Conquering Lion of Judah', 'King of Zion', 'Negus Nagast' (King of Kings) and Emperor of Ethiopia. I was in his presence about half-a-dozen times. I did exchange a few words with him. He had an aura and a persona which few of his peers could match. He was only five feet one inch tall. His build was ectomorphic. Authority cascaded effortlessly. His postures were royal. He was a part of history. No other African leader could make a similar claim (Mandela came on the scene much later).

In the summer of 1962, the UN committee on decolonization visited Morocco, Ethiopia and Tanzania. I was rapporteur of the committee. Its task was to meet petitioners from non-self-governing territories. These petitioners could not afford to fly to New York to appear before the committee. The list of the countries to be visited by the committee was carefully drawn up. Ethiopia was the headquarters of the Organization of African Unity (OAU). It was the oldest independent country on the African continent. It had never

K. Natwar Singh in Addis Ababa, 1962.

President Mandela Sir,
Do you still get
up at 3 A.M.?
Natwar Singh
at about 4.30 am
– N Mandela
27.1.95

The author's note to Nelson Mandela.

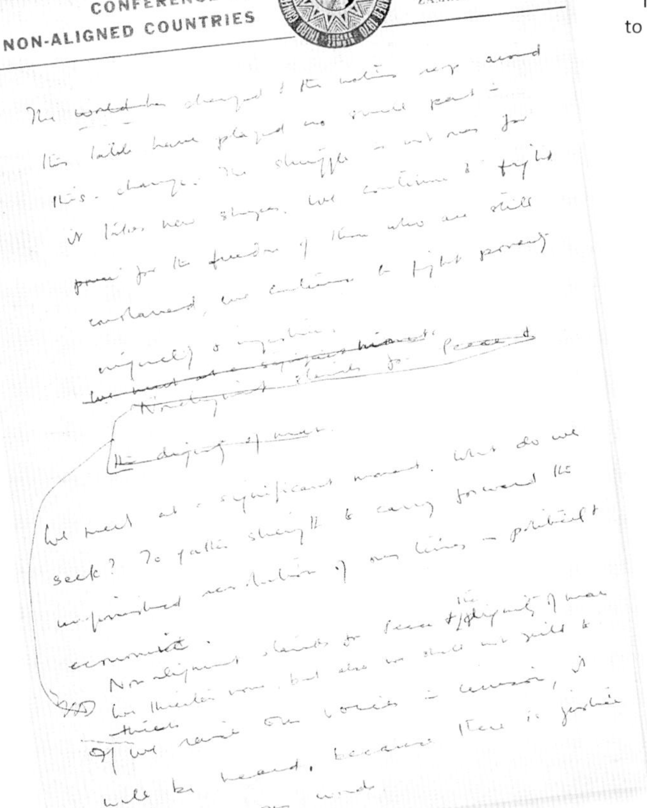

THIRD
CONFERENCE OF
NON-ALIGNED COUNTRIES

LUSAKA
ZAMBIA

Indira Gandhi's speech at the NAM summit, Lusaka, 1970.

The author with Queen Elizabeth II and Indira Gandhi at Rashtrapati Bhavan, 1983.

'Frontier Gandhi' Khan Abdul Ghaffar Khan sharing the dais with Rajiv Gandhi at the 1985 Congress centenary celebrations, Mumbai. Between them is Mohammad Yunus.

Jawaharlal Nehru with his two sisters, Krishna Hutheesing (left) and Vijayalaksmi Pandit (second from left). Also in the picture is a young Indira Gandhi (right).

Prime Minister Indira Gandhi with the PLO chairman, Yasser Arafat, at the 1983 NAM summit in New Delhi.

Prime Minister Indira Gandhi used to take commercial flights for her international trips.

Chandraswami, the controversial godman.

'Iron lady' Margaret Thatcher was the prime minister of the UK for eleven years, as predicted by Chandraswami.

Prime Minister Rajiv Gandhi and US president Ronald Reagan got along on first-name terms, though there was a gap of thirty-three years between them. Here seen at the White House during Rajiv's 1987 US visit.

Indira Gandhi with US president Richard Nixon at the White House, 1970. The two were not on the best of terms.

The author with Prime Minister Indira Gandhi and Pakistani president General Zia-ul Haq at the NAM summit, New Delhi, 1983.

The author with Russian president Vladimir Putin and Sonia Gandhi in Saint Petersburg, Russia, 2005.

S. Radhakrishnan greets Chairman Mao. The vice-president was received by the top Chinese leadership on his arrival in Beijing, 1957.

Cuban prime minister Fidel Castro embracing Rajiv Gandhi. Rajiv is accompanied by his wife Sonia Gandhi and Foreign Minister K. Natwar Singh. Havana, 1988.

The author at the 1983 NAM summit, Vigyan Bhavan.

King Birendra of Nepal. India had a tough time negotiating with him.

General Vo Nguyen Giap, hero of Vietnam's independence struggle, greeting the author in Hanoi, 1984.

The first president of Tanzania, Julius Nyerere.

President Seretse Khama, under whom Botswana went through rapid economic and social progress.

Kwame Nkrumah, the first president and prime minister of Ghana.

Hastings Banda ruled Malawi with an iron fist for thirty years.

Foreign Minister K. Natwar Singh shared a warm relationship with Zambian president Kenneth Kaunda.

A young Dalai Lama meeting Nehru soon after his arrival in India.

The author with noted writer Nirad C. Chaudhuri at the latter's home in Oxford.

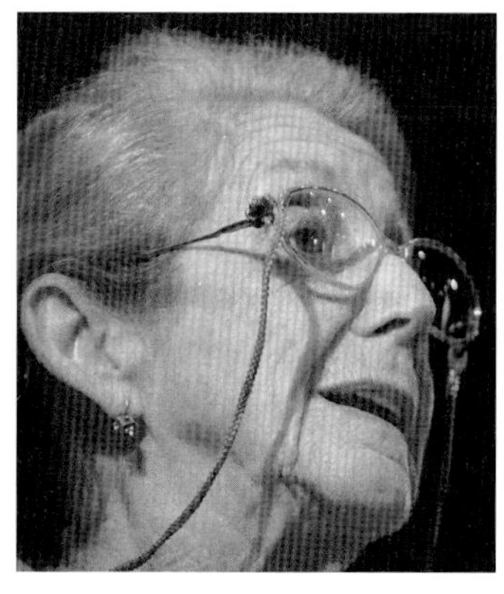
South African writer and activist Nadine Gordimer, who received the Nobel Prize in Literature in 1991.

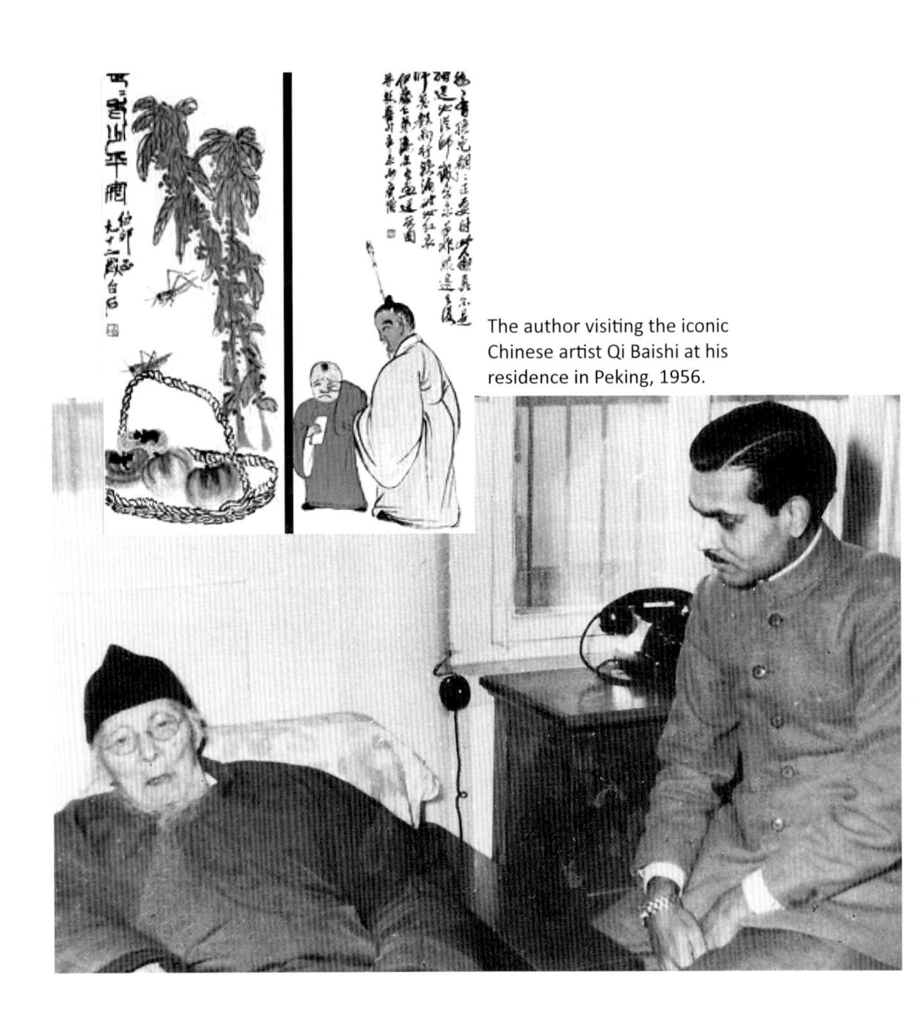

The author visiting the iconic Chinese artist Qi Baishi at his residence in Peking, 1956.

Legendary painter M.F. Husain paints his friend in New York, 1963.

been conquered except by Italy in 1935. That conquest ended in 1941 when the British expelled the Italian occupiers. Emperor Haile Selassie had spent five years in Bath in England and returned to reclaim his throne.

Addis Ababa, Ethiopia's capital, lies at an elevation of 7,546 feet. The airport was not impressive. More goats than human beings were to be seen. Our audience with His Imperial Majesty was scheduled for the next afternoon. The Ethiopian delegate in the committee, Kifle Wodajo, instructed us on the elaborate palace protocol.

We arrived at the grand palace and were awestruck by the lions walking unconcerned in the vast palace grounds. The committee members were taken to a large hall. No chairs. We stood, knowing not what to expect next. The emperor suddenly appeared, looking rather stiff in his military uniform. All Ethiopians present, including Kifle Wodajo, prostrated before him. His Imperial Majesty's entourage included a chihuahua who was shown due reverence by our hosts. We later discovered that the choice of the tiny canine was deliberate. Our committee came very low in the Ethiopian pecking order and did not merit a bigger canine presence. Before we filed past, His Imperial Majesty said a few words in Amharic and wished our delegation well. Kifle Wodajo was last in the line. He crawled, lowered his head and walked backwards so as not to show his posterior to the King of Kings.

In Addis Ababa I was staying with Ambassador R.G. Rajwade, who I had known for many years. He belonged to Gwalior and was inducted into the IFS in October 1948. He was a mildly rumbustious individual. I related to him the committee's audience with His Majesty and the antics of the little chihuahua. He then related this priceless story.

In Ethiopia the presentation of credentials ceremony was an elaborate affair. The imperial protocol for ambassadors was rigorously starchy and stiff. The emperor sat on his gold throne. On each side was a lion which the emperor patted from time to time. At the end of the ceremony, the ambassador was escorted by the chief of protocol, with the two lions following. At this stage most ambassadors panicked. Not the Indian ambassador. Rajwade walked on nonchalantly. This was a test of nerves and he did not let the side down.

This was too much for the chief of protocol. He asked Rajwade, 'Excellency, do you see the two lions following you?' His Excellency Ambassador Ramchandra Ganpat Rajwade responded, 'Excellency, I have not noticed them. My humble eyes were fixed on His Imperial Majesty Negus Nagast, King of Kings.' Touché. From then on the Indian ambassador was treated with respect if not reverence.

Indira Gandhi met the emperor twice, once in Delhi and the other time at Lusaka, at the NAM summit. Nothing of great significance transpired except that the emperor asked the PM to let our military personnel to continue to train Ethiopian army officers.

The emperor had a gruesomely tragic end. He was dethroned by the army, and on 27 August 1975 was smothered to death with a wet pillow and buried beneath a palace lavatory.

Two of his granddaughters were imprisoned in a filthy dungeon, and their heads shaved. This was on 11 September

1975. In October Winston Churchill Jr, MP and grandson of Sir Winston Churchill, met me at India House (in London). He spoke of the terrible plight of the princesses and wondered if Prime Minister Indira Gandhi could impress upon the army regime to release them. I informed the PM. She did discreetly intervene on purely humanitarian grounds and they were allowed to leave Ethiopia. Both were released and flew to England. Thus ended the oldest dynasty in the world, older than that of Japan.

29

The King of Nepal and I

Large countries like India need to be extra careful in their dealings with smaller neighbours. Their political egos and sensitivities must be borne in mind all the time. The Nepalese monarchy was an extreme case of excessive touchiness. It invented slights where none existed.

During the NAM summit in March 1983, His Majesty's tantrums caused Indira Gandhi considerable irritation. For reasons beyond her control, the time of her call on the king had to be changed—as were the calls on the presidents of Cuba, Tanzania, Egypt and Zambia. She had been meeting dozens of heads of government, and the demands on her time caused this change. No one else objected to a brief postponement of a one-on-one meeting. Except the king of Nepal (more so his courtiers), who took this as a slight. The Nepalese ambassador held me responsible for Mrs Gandhi's discourtesy 'to my King', and it took me quite some time to convince our Nepalese friends.

The monarchy was dealt a fatal blow when an erratic and inebriated Prince Dipendra shot his parents and close family members in 2001. Successive kings had surrounded themselves with advisers who were inspired intriguers, dedicated sycophants and conscientious frauds. They ill-served their unsuspecting masters, who, alas, always missed the pulse of time.

In 1988 Indo-Nepalese relations took a nosedive. Nepalese embassies in different parts of the world (especially at the UN) were badmouthing India and ineptly playing the China card. For several months we did not react.

By the middle of 1988 Prime Minister Rajiv Gandhi had had enough of the imaginary grievances of the Nepali establishment. I was at the time minister of state for external affairs. The PM asked me to go to Kathmandu and have a meeting with His Majesty King Birendra. This I did on 22 July 1988 in a small RAW airplane. I met the king the same afternoon. No one else was present.

After conveying the greetings of the prime minister, I said that we attached the highest importance to Indo-Nepalese relations which we cherished and valued. However, lately, we were getting mixed signals from Kathmandu. And it had become imperative to address them. Mr Gandhi had asked me to ascertain 'From Your Majesty if you intend to restructure or remould our bilateral relations'. The king said this was not so and hence there was no need to 'review our relations with India'. I thanked His Majesty but sought his permission to speak frankly and place before him some facts of which he might not be aware.

Even though Indian bids for several internationally funded projects in Nepal were the lowest, these were not awarded to India. India fulfilled all the conditions laid down by the World Bank. A bid for a paper project in the Terai too was rejected.

Under the 1950 Indo-Nepal Treaty of Peace and Friendship it was obligatory for His Majesty's government to inform us of the details of the military equipment Nepal wished to buy from a third country. We knew that such military supplies had been obtained from another country. This was against the letter and spirit of the treaty. I asked His Majesty why Nepal needed anti-aircraft guns. The answer was bordering on the farcical, 'These were to be used to fight the terrorists.'

I did not press the point that we could supply all the arms Nepal required. His Majesty next inquired if India could help Nepal in raising two mountain divisions in the next ten years. I told him that I would convey the king's request to the prime minister.

Next I took up the issue of work permits. Why were Indians required to have work permits? No Nepali in India required permits. His Majesty was cordial, even friendly. Unfortunately he was not forthright.

I next took up the vital question regarding the 1950 treaty itself. From time to time rumours (perhaps planted) emanated from responsible quarters that the 1950 Indo-Nepal Treaty of Peace and Friendship should be revised or done away with. That was Nepal's prerogative. We would respect the decision of his government. I, however, told the king that as a friend and well-wisher of Nepal, it was my duty to place some hard facts before him.

India could live without the treaty. Could Nepal? Once the treaty was abrogated, certain adverse consequences would follow. Millions of Nepalese living in India *could* be asked to apply for work permits. The passport issue could not be avoided. Transit preferences—trains, etc.—could be withdrawn. The highly objectionable activities of a very close relative of His Majesty *could* come under close scrutiny. I continued: 'I have mentioned some of the issues because the prime minister instructed me to do so. India has a special relationship with Nepal. Jawaharlal Nehru had declared in Parliament that India's defence line was on the Nepal–Tibet border. Both countries were tied by religion and culture and much else ...'

The king said that he appreciated my being sent by the PM to meet him. No misunderstandings existed. 'You can assure the prime minister that I have no intention of reviewing, revising or abrogating the 1950 treaty.'

It was a sensitive mission. No publicity was given. Did it produce the desired results? Not wholly. On some matters His Majesty dragged his royal feet. He prevaricated. Only after Rajiv Gandhi's prolonged meeting with King Birendra at the NAM summit in Belgrade in 1989 did India–Nepal relations take a turn for the better—at least for some time.

30

The Road to Mandalay

Burma was a part of the British Indian Empire till 1937. Bal Gangadhar Tilak spent six years in Mandalay jail. Subhash Chandra Bose too spent several years in that mosquito-ridden, ill-kept establishment. I paid an official visit to Burma in September 2004. While in Mandalay I visited the jail compound. The jail has been pulled down but the twelve-feet-high sinister walls were a grim reminder of Britain's brutal Burma.

With the military coup in 1962, Burma turned its back on the world. Now there is a break in the dark clouds in the Burmese sky. The military junta has had to make unheard of democratic concessions. After two decades of house arrest, the charismatic and gutsy Aung San Suu Kyi is leading her party in the elections. Her father, Aung San, was assassinated in 1947. He was thirty-four years old and led Burma's freedom movement. Had he lived, he would have become independent Burma's first prime minister.

Burma remained a democracy till 1962. That year General Ne Win ousted Prime Minister U Nu, and the travails and trials of the people of Burma began. Their agony lasted far too long—forty-nine years. Ne Win was a Buddhist who flouted the basic tenets of a great religion. India had no choice but to deal with his government.

In the latter half of 1987, Prime Minister Rajiv Gandhi paid an official visit to Burma. I accompanied him. He had done his homework and looked forward to his talks with General Ne Win and other leaders. It was his desire to put some life into the Indo-Burmese relations. Burma was rich in timber, oil, jewels and rice. India could help Burma all across the board.

The airport welcome was austerely friendly. No large crowds, no cheering. In the evening the PM called on General Ne Win. He was accompanied by Foreign Secretary K.P.S. Menon, Ambassador I.P. Singh and myself. General Ne Win had brought two gentlemen with him. I recognized the foreign minister. The identity of the other dignitary was soon known. The general said, 'Rajiv, this is the president of Burma. He normally talks very little. In my presence he does not talk at all.' His Excellency the President did not let Ne Win down. For the next hour he did not utter a word.

From the word go General Ne Win adopted an avuncular tone. Every proposal the prime minister made was brushed aside. Tourism. 'I dislike tourists. They give wrong ideas to our people. I made a big mistake by allowing Germany to open a tourist office. I am going to have it closed,' the general announced. Before the prime minister could make a proposal to increase trade, the general lapsed into nostalgia. 'Rajiv, you must have been very young when I met your grandfather.' Yes, he was young. Rajiv ignored the general's nostalgia. India could train Burmese technicians, give scholarship to students, Rajiv Gandhi proposed. The answers were not encouraging. 'When students go abroad, they get fancy ideas. I remember a talk with your mother about this.' Rajiv Gandhi kept his cool. I could see he was driven to controlled indignation. It was, to say the least, a frustrating experience.

Later, there was a meeting with the Burmese PM and several other ministers. Each proposal made by Rajiv Gandhi was joyfully accepted. What a contrast! What fruitful discussions!

Our joy was short-lived. General Ne Win would have none of it. He overruled his prime minister. Nothing in my diplomatic experience had prepared me for so bizarre an encounter.

Finally, Burma is stepping out of a long and dark tunnel, and breathing the fresh breeze of democracy. Aung San Suu Kyi has been in the forefront of this battle for democracy. She is an authentic hero. She is an inspiration. In 1995 the Indira Gandhi Memorial Trust awarded Suu Kyi the Indira Gandhi Prize for Peace. She could not attend as she was not allowed to leave Rangoon. I went to Oxford to meet her husband, Dr Michael Aris, to invite him to New Delhi to receive the prize. Alas! He too could not come.

Suu Kyi finally came to India in November 2012 to deliver the Nehru Memorial Lecture and received a standing ovation.

31

The Forgotten Cause Célèbre

The British Empire in Africa was vast. The three British protectorates in southern Africa included Bechuanaland. It became Botswana in 1966 on attaining independence. Its area is 231,804 square miles. Almost half is taken up by the Kalahari Desert. In the north-west are the Okavango Swamps, famous for wildlife and a paradise for ornithologists.

The chief who put Bechuanaland on the map was Khama III—born in 1830, and died in 1923. His descendant was Sir Seretse Khama (1921–80), who became the founding president of Botswana. His family was the head of the Bamangwato tribe. The chieftainship was hereditary.

As a future chief Khama was given the best possible education. He was sent to Balliol College, Oxford. While in England he fell in love with an English girl, Ruth Williams, and married her in 1949. All hell broke loose. One of the most bizarre and noisy cause célèbre entered history books.

The marriage was condemned by Khama's formidable uncle, Chief Tshekedi Khama. The white racists were outraged and bayed for Khama's blood. How could a black man's white wife become 'queen' in their region, southern Africa, where mixed marriages constituted a crime? In London the Labour government of Clement Attlee behaved abominably. Khama was deprived of his claim to chieftainship, and not allowed to return home. He had friends in the Labour party. Fenner Brockway was the most vocal supporter, but he made no headway.

Eventually, the 'winds of change' brought Sir Seretse back home, a hero. His wife won the hearts of the Bamangwato people.

The British African Empire dissolved at an astonishingly rapid pace. Between 1947 and 1957 India, Pakistan, Burma, Ceylon, Israel, Jordan and Malaya gained independence. Between 1958 and 1970 Singapore, Zambia, Kenya, Tanzania, Botswana, Uganda, Fiji and Cyprus followed. It was almost a case of cut and run. I distinctly remember President Julius Nyerere of Tanzania saying to me, 'We did not expect Britain to leave Tanganyika before 1975. But in fact, we were a free country by 1961.'

As high commissioner to Zambia I was also accredited to the Republic of Botswana, already a flourishing democracy under the benign and wise rule of Sir Seretse Khama. The per capita income was $1,500. I flew to Gaborone, the capital, in a ramshackle Dakota. I was to present my credentials to President Khama. It was November 1977. We stopped on the way at Francistown—a barren, inhospitable place. Not a soul in sight. My enthusiasm subsided. The weather made up for these short annoyances. It was the end of autumn, nippy but comfortable.

Gaborone revived our spirits; my wife accompanied me. The town's population was a little over 100,000. All things that were not available in Lusaka could be bought in the capital of Botswana. The South African border was less then twenty-five kilometres away. We decided to take a drive to the frontier. On the way a huge African elephant appeared and blocked the road. The driver said we had to be silent and wait. The majestic mammal would take its time to decide whether to attack our vehicle or ignore us and walk away. African elephants are much bigger than ours and cannot be trained. Since the massive quadruped did not budge, we ultimately turned around and got back to Gaborone before dark.

Soon after my arrival, the protocol office of the president informed me that my credentials ceremony was to be held the next day at 10 a.m. I had brought my speech for the occasion with me from Lusaka. The next morning, I dressed up in my *achkan* and *churidar* pyjamas. My wife and I arrived at the State House a few minutes before 10 o' clock. I was ushered into the president's austere office. My wife was escorted to Lady Khama's drawing room.

Sir Seretse Khama was broad of body. His complexion was dark brown. His smile was radiant. He greeted me affably. 'Welcome to Botswana, Your Excellency. I gather you are the first Asian diplomat to set foot on our soil. We Africans have high regard for Gandhi and Nehru, who inspired us. Welcome. Do sit down.' He made me feel at home. His aristocratic ease of manner one could not but notice. First impressions can be deceptive. This time it was not so. I was in the presence of a man of charm, distinction and substance.

'You have your speech ready, Excellency, I presume.' 'Yes, Excellency, I do.' 'So do I,' said Sir Khama. I was all ready to deliver my diplomatic masterpiece when to my utter surprise he said, 'Let's cut out this protocol business. Give me your speech. Here's mine. You are now high commissioner of India to Botswana. Let's join the ladies for tea.' I was bowled over. It was the shortest, refreshingly novel and memorable credentials ceremony of my career.

Formality was abandoned but familiarity was not entertained. We both knew where to draw the line.

32

Instant Diplomacy at Harare

Iran's impact on India has been manifold and multi-layered. This is particularly true of north India. Our culture, languages, art, architecture, cuisine, attire, literature and poetry owe much to Iran. All this in spite of Nadir Shah's 'terrible visitation' in 1738–39

My first visit to Iran was in 1982, as secretary general designate of the seventh NAM summit to be held in New Delhi in March 1983. I asked my hosts to arrange for me to see their renowned treasury which housed some of the most precious collection of jewels in the world. The guide who showed me around calmly announced that almost half of what was on display was the 'loot' Nadir Shah had brought from India! Sightseeing was not my main objective, although I did go to the holy city of Qom. My main mission was to seek an audience with Ayatollah Khameini, number two in the all-powerful religious hierarchy of Iran.

Meeting the Ayatollah was a rare honour. I briefed him on the arrangements that were under way for the seventh NAM summit. He heard me out. In all seriousness he asked me to tell Mrs Indira Gandhi that she should not invite Iraq to the summit. Respectfully I told him that as chairperson designate of the summit, she could not do so for the simple reason that Iraq would/could ask for Iran to be excluded. He got the point. What still remains is my memory is his composure. Authority emanated from every pore. He was serene. His austere grandeur was all too visible. His dignity and regal demeanour stood out.

We were to meet again three years later in Harare. This time I had a secondary but not an entirely insignificant role. Prime Minister Rajiv Gandhi was to hand over the chairmanship of the NAM to Prime Minister Robert Mugabe of Zimbabwe. This was Rajiv Gandhi's first NAM summit. His was a refreshingly new voice in the international arena. He presided over the opening session. Mugabe sat to his right. One of the morning's speakers was PLO leader Yasser Arafat. He made a blistering and unbridled attack on Iran. It was wholly unexpected and created a poor impression on most delegates. At this level and on such occasions, leaders usually use restrained language. Arafat had crossed the diplomatic *lakshmana rekha*.

During the lunch break we learnt that the Ayatollah, who was leading the Iranian delegation, would be exercising his right of reply in response to Arafat's outburst. This he would in the afternoon session when Rajiv Gandhi would be handing over the chairmanship to Mugabe.

How were we to deal with so hot a NAM potato? A public

row between Iran and the Palestine Liberation Organization leader, on the very first day, would inevitably cast a shadow on the proceedings. The media would make the most of it. Rajiv Gandhi consulted senior members of his delegation, which included External Affairs Minister P. Shiv Shankar, K.R. Narayanan, Mohammad Yunus, additional secretary, external affairs, and a close friend of the Nehru family, and myself. It was apparent that unless we acted quickly, the law of unintended consequences would take over. I suggested to Rajiv Gandhi that he ask to meet the Ayatollah to request him not to exercise his right of reply. Mine was not a win–win proposal. I was putting my neck on the line. If the Ayatollah agreed to meet the PM but rejected his appeal, my position would become untenable. But a more serious result would be for the summit to commence on an acrimonious note.

Rajiv Gandhi was a risk-taker. At the same time, he was not given to taking unnecessary risks. He had, however, in less than a year learnt that diplomacy was about conciliation, consultation and cooperation. He gave me the green signal to go to the Ayatollah. I embarked on a mission hoping the lights would not turn red. The spiritual leader heard me out. A terse but positive response relieved me no end. He would certainly receive the prime minister.

Ronen Sen, the IFS colleague working in the PM's office, and I accompanied Rajiv Gandhi to this crucial meeting. With disarming candour he said he had come to ask a favour. That broke the ice. The Ayatollah smiled. He would do what he could to oblige the prime minister. Rajiv Gandhi said, 'Your Excellency, I am told you would be exercising your right to reply to Mr Arafat's speech.' The Ayatollah said he intended doing so. Rajiv Gandhi asserted that what the PLO leader had said was unacceptable, and that he fully appreciated the Ayatollah's decision to reply to Arafat. However, his right of reply would inevitably make Arafat exercise his right of reply, which he was entitled to under the rules. In such a situation the summit would begin on a very disruptive note. The Iranian asked what the PM wished him to do. Rajiv Gandhi said he had come not as outgoing chairman or as a prime minister, but as a friend and well-wisher of Iran. He held the Ayatollah in high esteem. Would he consider not replying to Arafat and save the summit? This was the favour he had come to ask. I watched the Ayatollah. His expression gave nothing away. We waited. With a slight smile and a twinkle in his eye the great man pronounced his decision: 'If the prime minister of India, our friend, desires that we not exercise our right of reply, we shall not do so.' These may not be the exact words but they are near enough. This was a memorable triumph of diplomacy at the highest level. Youth and age connected. The summit was saved.

33
The Wrong Road

In November 1986 Mikhail Gorbachev, general secretary of the Communist Party of the USSR, paid a landmark visit to India. The high point of his journey was to sign the Delhi Declaration with Rajiv Gandhi on 27 November 1986. It is now only of archival interest. Much time was spent in preparing the agreed text for the two leaders to put their seal on in the declaration. A number of principles were enunciated in the transcript: 'Human life must be acknowledged as the supreme value ... non-violence must become the basis of human coexistence ...'

Here was the general secretary of the Communist Party of the Soviet Union accepting non-violence as a necessary ingredient for running the global system. This was unprecedented. Rajiv Gandhi and Gorbachev established a warm personal rapport. It was in a way a fresh endeavour to energize the Indo-Soviet friendship. This was necessary to put behind the sloth of the arid years of Leonid Ilyich Brezhnev and his two immediate successors, Yuri Andropov and Konstantin Chernenko.

Comrade Andropov lasted less than two years; Comrade Chernenko not even a year.

The Mikhail–Rajiv *jugalbandi*, alas, was not fated to last long. Rajiv Gandhi was assassinated on 21 May 1991. Gorbachev was overthrown six months later. Nevertheless, between November 1986 and May 1991, intense diplomatic activity was in evidence on both sides. Among the more significant events was the visit of the Russian prime minister, Nikolai Ryzhkov, a close ally of Gorbachev. Ryzkov was not a heavyweight politician—not in the same league as Gorbachev. He was received at Palam airport by the PM and the usual assortment of ministers, service chiefs, the police commissioner and others.

It was early October. Winter was hovering around. The two prime ministers decided to drive together to Rashtrapati Bhavan. I took a lift with Ved Marwah, the Delhi police commissioner. We had known each other since our days at St Stephen's College. He had done his bit to get me elected as president of the college union. I had to get back to South Block quickly to collect my briefs for the meeting of the two delegations, and then rush to Hyderabad House. The fastest way was to ride in the commissioner's car, to overcome traffic hold ups.

We arrived at South Avenue and then drove towards the south of Rashtrapati Bhavan, then turned right to take the road leading to South Block. Here disaster struck. We saw the carcade of the two prime ministers coming from the opposite direction. Ved Marwah asked his driver to reverse gear to get out of the way. In a few seconds the carcade would be within a few yards of us. Right behind us was the late Bhajan Lal's car. It took half a minute to reverse both cars. We avoided the carcade by a hair's breath.

Rapid-fire events followed. The prime minister asked the home minister Buta Singh to suspend Ved Marwah. I came to know of this a few hours later. At lunch the PM walked up to me and gave me a well-deserved tongue lashing: 'Don't look so innocent. The commandos could have shot you for breaking the strict security regulations.' The PM was livid. I had the good sense to keep my mouth shut. A prime ministerial raspberry in public is a most disagreeable experience. The news spread. I felt rotten about landing Ved in serious trouble.

A day or two later, I saw the PM in his office in Parliament. I said how sorry I was for so serious a security lapse. If any one deserved to be chastized, it was me. Ved Marwah was not at fault. I was. I had asked him to make sure that I got to South Block before the prime ministers reached Rashtrapati Bhavan. He could hardly have declined. I was, after all, a minister.

Rajiv Gandhi heard me out. He was indifferent. He was still annoyed. Justifiably so. Later I spoke to Sarla Grewal, the principal secretary to the PM. I told her Ved had been unfairly treated. This gross injustice had to be rectified. Marwah was an outstanding officer with an unblemished service record. The home minister, I gathered, was in no hurry to get Ved off the hook. In purgatory Ved conducted himself with stoic dignity and took the rap in his stride. I kept in touch with him, apologizing profusely.

The dust settled down by the end of the week. I saw the PM once more. He graciously relented. Ved Marwah was back at work. He ended his career as governor of Manipur, Mizoram and then Jharkhand. Now, when we meet, we laugh recalling the incident. In October 1987 it was not a laughing matter.

34

The Sardar Outwits Bhutto

Jawaharlal Nehru, the idealist, took the Kashmir issue to the UN Security Council in good faith in December 1947. By doing so he converted an internal matter into an international one. He compounded this serious error of judgement by approaching the Security Council under Chapter VI of the UN charter, which is concerned with the 'Pacific Settlement of Disputes'. We should have approached the Security Council under Chapter VII. Article 39 of the chapter reads: 'The Security Council shall determine the existence of any threat to the peace, breach of the peace, or act of aggression and shall make recommendations, or decide what measures shall be taken … to maintain or restore international peace and security.'

The decision to refer Kashmir to the Security Council was taken by Nehru on the advice of Mountbatten. While Sardar Patel was in charge of the princely states, the state of Jammu and Kashmir was the responsibility of Nehru.

In a letter to Sheikh Abdullah, dated 10 October 1947, Nehru wrote: 'For me Kashmir's future is of the most intimate personal significance.' At the Security Council, from day one, the dice was loaded against us. Britain openly sided with Pakistan. The US followed the UK. Nehru was dismayed and disgusted. Kashmir became a victim of Cold War pulls and pressures. The Security Council ignored India's complaint about Pakistani aggression in Kashmir, and converted the Kashmir question into the 'Indo-Pak question'.

A meeting was called by Lord Mountbatten on 25 February 1948 to discuss Kashmir. Those present were Nehru, Patel, Mountbatten, Gopalaswami Ayyangar and Patrick Gordon-Walker, a member of Attlee's government. I found his presence an infringement on India's sovereignty. These meetings should have been presided over by Nehru. Mountbatten's record of the meeting is most revealing:

> Nehru said that it had been an act of faith by the Government of India, at a time when the situation was rapidly deteriorating, to make their reference to the Security Council in the first place. If this faith was now proved to be misplaced, the consequences would have to be borne by those who had made the reference ... Patel said that Nehru in particular had great faith in the institution of the UNO. But the Security Council had been meddling in power politics to such an extent that very little of this faith was left. He pointed out that it was the governor general who had induced the government to make the reference to the UNO in the first place.

Between 1948 and 1964 any numbers of meetings on Kashmir were held at the Security Council. In not a single one of them did India get a fair deal. The only beneficiary was the acerbic Krishna Menon, who became a hero in India after his nine-hour speech at the Council in 1956. However, members of the Security Council were not impressed. Their response in private was: 'If your case is so strong, than why is it necessary to take nine hours to explain it?' Indeed.

During 1964–65 several meetings of the Security Council were called to discuss the Kashmir question. The Indian ministers who participated in these meetings were Sardar Swaran Singh and M.C. Chagla. The Pakistani side was headed by Zulfikar Ali Bhutto. Singh and Bhutto had met earlier in Karachi, New Delhi and Kolkata. The contrast between them was all too obvious.

Sardar sahib was earthy, cautious, undramatic, steady, practical, sound, unflappable and lacking in the suave sophistication of Bhutto. He never got cold feet. Neither was he ever guilty of smashing the diplomatic crockery. He was reliable, with vast political experience. Prime Minister Lal Bahadur Shastri, to the surprise of almost every other Congress politician, had appointed him minister of external affairs in July 1964. The joke was that Swaran Singh did not know the difference between Ho Chi Minh and Aksai Chin. But he soon took the measure of his critics and made it abundantly clear that he did.

All his life Zulfikar Ali Bhutto lived on a political overdraft from a bank about to go bust. He was elegant, eloquent, sneering in tone, offensive in language. He was an intellectual, given to verbal typhoons. He lived on the edge.

The abyss awaited him. India, he loathed. A hedonist, he enjoyed the pleasures and prizes life offered. Bhutto was an exceptionally gifted diplomat. He befriended China without offending the Americans. He read widely. His library did him credit. He admired Nehru (in private) and respected S. Radhakrishnan.

During the Security Council debate, his schadenfreude was all too evident. He referred to Indians as 'dogs' and claimed that India had usurped Kashmir by devious, dishonest and foul means. On the surface it appeared that the simple Sardar Swaran Singh was no match for the ostentatious Pakistani. But he was soon to discover otherwise.

After the first day's session, members of the permanent mission of India led by Ambassador G. Parthasarathi, and including Brajesh Mishra, myself and S.K. Singh, suggested to the external affairs minister that if Mr Bhutto were to continue his unbridled tirade against India we should walk out of the Security Council. Neither Sardar sahib, nor the gentle, wise and level-headed G. Parthasarathi was given to diplomatic high jinks. Doing anything dramatic was not in their nature. But Parthasarathi was exasperated. And came around to the view that enough was enough and a walkout should be considered. Sardar Sahib was not wholly convinced. Such an act would be unprecedented and likely to be misunderstood. However, he could not ignore Parthasarathi's views. He had high regard for him. Sardar Swaran Singh was persuaded to call Lal Bahadurji to seek his permission. At that time, almost half-a-century back, it was not easy to call Delhi from New York. When Sardar sahib briefed the PM, Shashtriji's response was quintessentially diplomatic. He said to his minister, 'Sardar sahib, you are on the spot. Use your judgement.' Swaran Singh did precisely that. As soon as Bhutto began his verbal onslaught, the Indian delegation led by the external affairs minister staged a walkout.

An event so full of drama would normally have been on the front pages of all New York papers and on all TV channels. This did not happen. The walkout decision was a well-kept secret. No photographs exist. The debate fizzled out. The sting went out of the Kashmir issue at the UN. It remains on the UN agenda still, but there are no takers for it any more, thanks to Sardar Swaran Singh.

35

High Diplomatic Tantrum

The seventh NAM summit was to be held in Baghdad in September 1982. The Iraq–Iran war ruled out the Iraqi capital. The task fell on President Fidel Castro, chairman of the Non-Aligned Movement since 1979, to find a new venue. Several countries were willing to host the summit, including Indonesia and Yugoslavia. India did not canvass. Eventually Delhi was chosen. This was conveyed by President Castro to Prime Minister Indira Gandhi, who was to succeed him as chairperson at the seventh summit.

It usually takes almost two years to prepare for and organize a NAM summit. We were given less than six months. The date fixed was 7 March 1983. Real preparations began on 4 November, after the conclusion of the Asian Games. By any measure it was a gigantic undertaking. Mrs Gandhi selected me for the post of secretary general. It was a singular honour as I was the juniormost secretary in the Ministry of External Affairs. There was widespread scepticism regarding my credentials for so complex and demanding a job. I too had doubts. My only experience of summitry were the NAM summit in Lusaka, Zambia, in 1970, and the Commonwealth summit in Kingston, Jamaica, in 1975.

India had never played host to fifty or sixty heads of state and government, several vice-presidents, three kings—Bhutan, Jordan and Nepal—and over a hundred foreign ministers. It would have been a daunting task for anyone. And here was I, a novice, thrown among the high and the mighty. My benign stars helped me all the way. The shortage of time became a boon. The entire team, involving many ministries and departments, worked eighteen hours a day with dedication and vigorous determination and flawless precision.

The word got around that I had easy access to the PM. P.C. Alexander, her principal secretary, gave me unstinted support. Everything that could go right did go right. In a short while, the logistics were mastered. The renovation of Vigyan Bhavan was completed in record time. I was patting myself on the back when the PM dropped a bombshell. She sent for me and asked why the NAM leaders and their delegations could not be put up at the Asiad Village, near Siri Fort. The Asiad Village had been built for the Asian Games held in Delhi in 1982 to house the athletes. Not only would this save much expense, it would be welcomed by the security fraternity, as all delegates would be in one compound. I was dumbfounded. I thoughtlessly said, 'Madam, you can't be serious.' It was too late to retract so grave a folly. Her icy response was: 'Dear Mr Natwar Singh, I am very serious. Where do you think the money would come from? Why can't we do all this in an austere manner?' For good measure she added, 'My accommodation in Lusaka was nothing to write home about.' Some irresponsible individual had obviously misled the PM.

I respectfully said that Lusaka was not Delhi. Even in Zambia heads were put up in villas and not in university hostels. She was not convinced. A high-powered group visited the Asiad Village including Rajiv Gandhi. I succeed in convincing him that it would never do to put up kings, presidents and prime ministers at the Village. Even lesser mortals would object.

In the meanwhile, the heads of missions of non-aligned countries in New Delhi got wind of what was afoot. In clear terms they said: 'We hope the rumour about the Asiad Village is only a rumour. If not, then we are telling you that our presidents and prime ministers would not attend the summit.' This did the trick. Status quo ante was restored. But we had lost several days.

I visited a number of non-aligned capitals before the summit. By the end of February things had fallen into place. We had achieved an organizational miracle.

Several weeks before D-day many countries sent advance parties to scrutinize our security arrangements and seating plans. The North Korean deputy minister for security demanded that for President Kim Il Sung all streets leading to the hotel he was to stay in *must* be barricaded. The entire hotel *must* be put at the great leader's disposal. I told him that a uniform policy would be followed. No exceptions. Kim did not attend.

The late Saddam Hussein was to attend. He and his delegation would use two Boeing 747 planes. In which plane would he fly? No satisfactory answer was forthcoming from the Iraqi embassy in Delhi. Finally the Iraqi vice-president arrived. With him came dozens of armed commandos. They were disarmed, but not without a near confrontation.

On 7 March 1983 President Castro opened the summit. To his right was Indira Gandhi. I, to his left. That photograph appeared on the front page of thousands of newspapers all over the world including *The New York Times*, well known for its anti-Castro editorial policy.

The high-powered Cuban delegation included Gabriel Garçia Marquez, who had won the Nobel Prize for Literature six months earlier. Also present was Cuban vice-president Carlos Rafael Rodriguez, about whom the French president François Mitterrand had written in his book *The Wheat and the Chaff*: 'He became a Castroite without ceasing to be a Communist, while waiting for Fidel to become a Communist without ceasing to be a Castroite.'

After the opening ceremony, five leaders of delegations addressed the plenary session. Among them were the king of Jordan and the PLO leader Yasser Arafat. The session had concluded on an inspiring note.

Unsuspected trouble followed. S.K. Lamba, the deputy secretary general, came to me during the lunch break. 'Sir, we have a hell of a problem on our hands. Mr Arafat has just now informed us that he was insulted at the morning session by being asked to speak after King Hassan of Jordan. He has already alerted the crew of his aircraft. He would leave Delhi shortly.' I immediately informed Mrs Gandhi. I told her that since Castro was chairman till the afternoon session, she should take him into confidence. This she did. She arrived at Vigyan Bhavan in no time. President Castro joined her a few minutes later. He called Arafat to join them, and he came posthaste.

To watch Fidel Castro handle the temperamental Arafat was an education. He was mildly pugnacious. At the same time, he was amiable and prudent. He derived his authority from his character. He asked Arafat if he was a friend of Indira Gandhi's. The response was warm and genuine: 'Friend, she is my elder sister. I will do anything for her.' President Castro then admonished Arafat as if he was a university student. 'Then behave like a younger brother and attend the afternoon session.' Q.E.D. Arafat fell in line.

36

In and Out of the Stone Age

'Mr Singh, meet Blue Bird. He is just out of jail. He killed the man who was misbehaving with his lady. As soon as the deed was done, he came to the patrol officer and gave himself up.'

This incident took place in the summer of 1964 in Papua New Guinea. What was I doing in this big and rugged island north of Australia? I was invited by the Australian government to spend ten days in Papua New Guinea. I was at the time rapporteur of the UN committee on decolonization. This territory was being administered by Australia. Strictly speaking, Australia was never a colonizing or imperialist country. Nevertheless, Papua New Guinea was included in the committee's agenda of non-self-governing territories.

For me this Australian outpost was virgin territory. All I knew was that it had been a part of the German Empire from 1884 to 1914. After World War I it came under Australian rule. New Guinea was rich in gold. Papua was not rich and even more inaccessible.

In Canberra we (the other committee member along with me was the representative from Iran) were briefed by the concerned officials looking after Papua New Guinea. Our first stop was at Port Moresby. We were invited to dinner by the governor. He and his wife had seen better days. They were in Port Moresby on sufferance. The wife was even more prickly about being dumped in a dump called Port Moresby. After dinner my Iranian colleague asked if he could use the toilet. He was admonished: 'Here, we do not ask to use a toilet. We say, "Can I go for a walk?"'

Next day, we embarked on our passage to the unknown and the unseen. A four-seater Cessna aircraft was at our disposal. We were, to our great surprise, informed that in Papua New Guinea, one either walked or flew. No roads existed. The terrain was covered by very thick impenetrable forest. No horses. Neither cows, buffalos or deer. Only pigs, introduced by the Japanese during World War II. (However the country is an ornithologist's paradise.)

Our first halt was at Mt Hagen, 6,000 feet above sea level. Our tiny plane was flying at 8,000 feet. 'Fasten your seat belts, we are about to land.' I looked for an airport. None was to be seen. The plane came down on an uneven field, not much bigger than a football pitch. It halted a few yards away from the edge of a deep gorge. We were to spend the night with the commissioner, who received us at the 'airport'. I do not remember his name. He was dressed as a *pukka sahib*, in khaki shirt and shorts, matching stockings and a felt hat that one saw the Gurkhas wearing. After dinner he gave us a fascinating briefing on life in the island, its fauna and flora, its geography, the life of the people, aborigines, Polynesians, their ways of living.

He was the only white man within 200 miles. His sole contact with the world was by a radio set, a device to keep in touch with Port Moresby. Often these did not function. He spoke the local language fluently. Casually he informed us that the island had seven thousand languages—not dialects, mind you! Without being patronizing, he said the Australian policy might smack of paternalism but it was committed to bringing a Stone Age people into the twentieth century. The people were primitive, their customs barbaric. They believed in a supernatural world of devils, spirits, sorcery and ghosts. They used bows and arrows with deadly accuracy. Their diet was simple—cocoa, millet, sago, pigs and fruit. Betel nut chewing was endemic. No sexual taboos; occasionally jealousy led to cannibalism and murder. Their life had remained static for thousands of years. Neither men nor women wore any clothing.

Did the people wish to stay with Australia? The people did not.

Early next morning we flew to Goroka. The airfield was at a 30-degree angle. The plane landed and taxied up the hill. Then stopped. The village folk ran and placed stones behind the wheels, so that our aircraft would not slide down! A novel experience.

The sight we met was not something we were prepared for. The patrol officer, not more than twenty-five years of age, dressed in a white shirt, shorts and white stockings, took us to 'the school'. About twenty boys and girls were sitting at little desks reading a lesson in English. On the blackboard was written, 'Welcome to our guests'. Well, well. In this little room, in the middle of an inhospitable island, the Stone Age was meeting the twentieth century. A few of the parents of the children were looking at our plane, attired in almost nothing.

Our task began. We asked, through the interpreter, the assembled Kukukuku tribal leader, 'Would you like to live under Australia, or would you prefer self-determination or independence?' What followed was farcical. The interpreter translated our UN mandate into pidgin English for the benefit of the second interpreter, who in turn translated the pidgin into the region's language, who then asked the fourth interpreter to put it into the local dialect. The dozen or so natives heard him out, with incomprehension writ large on their faces.

The eldest one grunted a few words which got back to us via the serpentine translators' route: 'He asks if we could repeat our question?' We gave up. Yet, we were not wholly disappointed. We saw the future in the classroom. The weight of the past would be reduced soon. The Australians were dedicated, determined and driven. They had done much. Much more remained to be done.

Our last call was the coastal city of Rabaul, with a fine harbour and a not-too-intimidating volcano in the background. The climate was bracing. The grown-up sons of the hill tribes were running carpentry shops, first-aid stalls and other small-scale industries. The schools were full. The hospital was modern. Not far from Rabaul is the island of Guadalcanal where during World War II future president

John F. Kennedy's boat, PT-109, was sunk by the Japanese and he almost lost his life. Further down is Bougainville Island. The name of the flower originates from the island. A large white community populated the town. They were specimens of an era long over. Our mission was finally rewarded. In Rabaul we talked to men and women who were the first to be educated and had not abandoned their parents, their past or their tribe. Some were members of village councils and locally elected bodies. Yes, they were ready for self-rule. Fifteen years later, Papua New Guinea would become a member of the United Nations.

37

Radhakrishnan Surprises Mao

By the end of 1956 the momentous events in Egypt (the Suez crisis) and Hungary (the Hungarian revolution) were over. Sino-Indian relations were still in the 'Hindi Chini bhai-bhai' phase. Minor irritations on the border did not yet cause much worry on account of Chou En-Lai's assurances to Prime Minister Nehru. In December 1956, the Dalai Lama came to India for the Buddha Jayanti celebrations. Chou En-Lai was also in India, and did not take kindly to the warm reception given to His Holiness, who was keen to stay in India. Both prime ministers advised him to return to Tibet.

The rest of 1957 did not see any major public altercation between Beijing and New Delhi. The most spectacular event of the year was the space flight of the Russian satellite Sputnik. All of us in the embassy looked for it with our binoculars, but without success. It caused joy in Beijing and dismay in Washington. So did Khrushchev's divesting Comrades Lazar

Kaganovich, Georgy Malenkov and Vyacheslav Molotov of power.

In China the 'Hundred Flowers' campaign was launched, which allowed the people to freely express their views. The Great Leap Forward disaster was a couple of years away and the Cultural Revolution nine. In October Mao Zedong left Beijing for Moscow to participate in the fortieth anniversary of the Russian Revolution of 1917. The entire diplomatic corps was at the airport to see him off. He arrived wearing a solar hat which probably had accompanied the great man to Beijing from Yan'an.

Before leaving, Mao Zedong played host to Vice-president Radhakrishnan, who arrived in the Chinese capital on 18 September1957. At the airport he was received by the top Chinese leadership: Marshal Chu Teh, future president Liu Shaoqi, Chou En-Lai, Madam Soong Ching Ling, Marshals Chen Yi and Ho Lung, and the mayor of Beijing, Peng Zhen. This was a very great honour. The Chinese had done their homework. Radhakrishnan was for them not only the vice-president of India, but also a world-class philosopher. He had been ambassador to the Soviet Union between 1949 and 1952. The highlight of his Moscow stay was a meeting with Stalin, who had not received Mrs Vijayalakshmi Pandit, Radhakrishnan's predecessor. Normally, Stalin granted interviews late at night. For Radhakrishnan he set 9 p.m. He had also remarked, 'I would like to meet the ambassador who spends all his time in bed—writing.'

China had much appreciated Radhakrishnan's deploring the absence of the People's Republic of China from the UN.

From the airport the vice-president was driven to Chung Nan Hai, where Mao Zedong and other top leaders lived. I was attached to the vice-president's delegation which also included S. Gopal and Jagat Mehta. Radhakrishnan was put up in a house next to Mao's. I too managed to spend one night in this privileged abode. There was some speculation whether Chairman Mao would be in Beijing to receive Radhakrishanan. The guessing game was over. Mao returned to Beijing a day earlier.

Before writing about the vice-president's talks with the chairman, I must relate a remarkable incident. While Chou En-Lai had a way of entrancing people but being elastic at the same time, Mao Zedong was made of a different metal. No one disagreed with him. He had a powerful mind. He was a poet and a voracious reader. What was unique was his personal will, and that will he made sure was executed. Writer and Nobel Peace Prize recipient Henry Kissinger was mesmerized when he first met Mao. Theodore White, an American correspondent in China before 1949, has written that Mao's will, with the exception of Lenin, was the most formidable will of the twentieth century. Many world leaders called on Mao, including President Nixon. Mao never returned the compliment.

When Dr Radhakrishnan called on Mao Zedong, he was received in the courtyard of the chairman's house. Chou En-Lai was also present. After shaking hands, the vice-president patted Mao on his left cheek. The chairman had never been subjected to such familiarity. He was momentarily taken aback. The vice-president was quick to put Mao at ease by saying, 'Mr Chairman, don't be alarmed, I did the same thing to Stalin and the Pope.' What an exit line!

In the Mao–Radhakrishnan talks no serious problems were raised. Taiwan did figure. Dr Radhakrishnan said that the Taiwan problem would no doubt be solved peacefully. Time was on China's side. Mao made a startling observation. China was willing to wait a hundred years.

The vice-president asked about peaceful coexistence. Mao said he was for it. Dr Radhakrishnan was a bit didactic. The professor in him put aside the political nitty-gritties. To Dr Radhkrishnan's observation that if India and China stood together the world would take note of it, Mao said that if India and China stood together for twenty years, 'no one would be able to make us go on different paths'.

Twenty years were reduced to five, when China attacked India in 1962. But that is another story.

38

A Rendezvous with Nelson Mandela

> I have cherished the ideal of a democratic and free society in which all persons live together in harmony and with equal opportunities. It is an ideal which I hope to live for and to achieve. But if needs be, it is an ideal for which I am prepared to die.
>
> Nelson Mandela
> 20 April 1964

Nelson Mandela is ninety-four now. He is the ultimate hero, admired, even venerated, around the world. Hemingway's definition of courage—'grace under pressure'—fits Mandela like a glove.

After he was released from jail on 11 February 1990, the government of V.P. Singh sent an additional secretary from the Ministry of External Affairs to convey India's greetings to the great man. It was an amazingly inadequate gesture on such a momentous occasion. Several of us in the Congress party suggested to Rajiv Gandhi that we send a high-powered Congress delegation to meet Mandela to felicitate him. Such a delegation was sent. P.V. Narasimha Rao, Anand Sharma and myself were selected for the purpose. I shall write about it some other time. Today I will recall Rajiv Gandhi's rendezvous with Nelson Mandela.

Namibia was to attain independence on 21 March 1990. India had vigorously supported the Namibian freedom struggle. We provided all the help we could, except supplying arms. Sam Nujoma, who would become the country's first president, was the undisputed leader of the freedom fighters. He had been to India several times. I had known him since my Lusaka days—1977–80. Rajiv Gandhi, though no longer prime minister, was invited to attend the independence day celebrations. He accepted the invitation and asked me to accompany him.

A major problem confronted us. How to get to Windhoek without touching South Africa. We had no diplomatic relations with it and had consistently condemned the imbecile racist follies of the South African regime. The only way South Africa could be bypassed was travelling via Lusaka. I telephoned President Kaunda of Zambia to inform him that Rajiv Gandhi would be halting in Lusaka on his way to Windhoek and would like to meet him. President Kaunda's response was heartwarming. 'Natwar, not only is Rajiv welcome, he must stay with me and fly to Windhoek with me in my personal plane.'

Rajiv Gandhi decided to travel economy class to Lusaka on a Zambian Airways flight. Soon after take off from Bombay, many passengers lined up to ask Rajiv Gandhi for his autograph. Commotion followed. The cabin crew complained that in such a situation they could not serve dinner. The purser very politely requested Rajiv Gandhi to shift to the fist-class cabin. I pleaded with him to accept this practical proposal. He would have none of it unless I and Gupta too were upgraded. (P.K. Gupta was his security officer. He was killed at Sriperumbudur—when Rajiv was assassinated.) The cabin staff immediately obliged.

When we landed at Lusaka airport, we were received by an official from State House, where we were to be put up. On arrival there Rajiv Gandhi was greeted by Kenneth Kaunda who escorted him to his suite. I got a room next to Rajiv.

For the next five days, Rajiv had to suffer my company. It was great fun being alone with him. It was also an unforgettable experience. The first thing I noticed about him was his implementation of the democracy of manners. He greeted everyone with a winning smile and a courtesy. He was totally unconcerned about rank. He used to get restless if he had nothing to do. He had brought a small radio with him. He installed an aerial in his room to hear BBC news. Kaunda treated him like a younger brother. He hosted a dinner for leaders of several countries who were travelling to Windhoek. I remember one in particular: Eduard Shevardnadze, the foreign minister of the USSR. When Rajiv Gandhi was PM, this man used to be excessively deferential. In Lusaka he hardly noticed us.

Rajiv met Nelson Mandela on the morning of 21 March 1990. We were in our *bandgallas* awaiting our brush with history. Nelson Mandela greeted him with affection and warmth. Rajiv Gandhi's opening words were: 'Mr Mandela, when my daughter learnt that I would be meeting you, she made me promise that when I shook hands with you, I should think of her. This I am doing now.' Mandela enjoyed that very much. Pleasantries did not take much time. Rajiv asked about the situation in South Africa. Before answering Mandela recalled the support of the Congress party during his imprisonment. About the future he was realistic. Much needed to be done. He wanted to bring in the whites on board. Negotiations with President F.W. de Klerk (he was also in Windhoek; Rajiv Gandhi met him briefly) would be complicated and prolonged. No government gives up power easily. He himself was catching up with all that had transpired during his incarceration.

I listened spellbound. Here was real greatness. No rancour. No bitterness. Elemental serenity combined with controlled passion. Rajiv Gandhi gave Mandela a tour de horizon of the Indian scene. Mandela listened with rapt attention. Rajiv asked him what his most urgent priority was. 'Reconciliation and reconstruction' was the reply. Such brevity. Such clear-headedness. It was an extraordinary summing up.

What we achieved on that momentous morning were rapport and understanding. Mandela at the time was in his seventy-second year; Rajiv Gandhi in his forty-fifth. The calendar difference in age was transcended in the first few minutes.

Mandela escorted Rajiv Gandhi to the car. Mrs Winnie Mandela joined us. She was ebullient, friendly and looked quite stunning. During the drive back Rajiv Gandhi and I did not talk. We were still breathing the Mandela aroma.

At the flag-raising ceremony on 21 March 1990, Rajiv Gandhi and I sat with the foreign ministers. The names of prominent leaders were called out. 'Mr Rajiv Gandhi, former prime minister of India.' He was semi-dozing. I gave him a nudge. He got up and waved. The audience applauded. Next 'His Excellency V.P. Singh, prime minister of India.' Silence. His name was called out a second time. No response. The prime minister had failed to make it to the venue on time!

39

A Distraught Begum

During my tenure as ambassador to Pakistan, I met Begum Nusrat Bhutto twice in private at her home in Clifton, Karachi.

Soon after taking up my post I learnt that the Indian embassy had no contact whatever with the Bhuttos. I was informed that Prime Minister Morarji Desai's instructions had been to keep away from Zulfikar Ali Bhutto's family. Morarji bhai was one of the very few heads of government who had not appealed to President Zia-ul-Haq to spare Bhutto's life. Indira Gandhi, then out of office, had appealed for mercy.

On my very first 'consultation' trip to New Delhi I apprised Prime Minister Indira Gandhi of this incongruity. I added that my counterpart in New Delhi—the Pakistani ambassador—frequently met Opposition leaders, media moguls, etc. I sought her permission to get in touch with the Bhuttos. Without a moment's hesitation she gave me the go-ahead.

The nervous system of Karachi was at the disposal of political warlords whose wealth made it unnecessary for them to pay heed to the squalour that surrounded their splendour. Their lifestyles made a mockery of the French and Russian revolutions. They all ate cakes. All were formidable politicians, chasing posts not principles. The most prominent was Zulfikar Ali Bhutto's widow, Begum Nusrat. President Zia-ul-Haq was the creation of Zulfikar Bhutto. The general had no hesitation in sending his mentor to the gallows. He reduced his widow to a non-person.

Getting in touch with Begum sahiba turned out to be a complicated and difficult undertaking. She was under intense surveillance. So was I. My deputy, Satti Lamba, had got to know Dr Niazi. He had been Bhutto's dentist and was a member of the Pakistan People's Party (PPP). I went to his clinic to have my teeth checked. I asked if he could arrange my meeting with Nusrat Bhutto. He gave no assurance but said he would try. He was taking a big risk.

After several false starts the meeting was fixed for 21 August 1981. I asked Mani Shankar Aiyar, our consul general in Karachi, to accompany me. We drove in his official car with the Indian flag flying. The drive took less than five minutes. The large gate was discreetly opened. We were ushered into a rectangular, well-appointed room. There were the two ladies, mother Nusrat, and the daughter Sanam. One could almost taste gloom. Sadness enveloped the duo. What once must have been the hub and home of gaiety and pleasure now offered the silence of the graveyard. One item stood out in the room: a striking lapis lazuli portrait of Zulfikar Ali Bhutto. The man had had taste.

Begum Nusrat Bhutto began by saying that at first she really did not believe that the Indian ambassador would come calling. Many busybodies had been conveying all kinds of messages. She thanked me for visiting her.

After handing over Mrs Gandhi's letter to her (it was to thank Mrs Bhutto for the condolences she had sent after Sanjay Gandhi's tragic death), I enquired about the political developments in Pakistan. She said that the Soviet intervention in Afghanistan in December 1979 had given legitimacy to Zia, which he did not have after hanging Chairman Bhutto. As a matter of fact, Zia had become an international outcaste. The ground reality was that there was widespread discontent. The high-handedness of the army was causing resentment. But she was pessimistic about any anti-Zia movement gathering support. He had skilfully divided or neutralized all political parties. She said, 'On the surface it looks that Zia-ul-Haq is in full control. It is true that Pakistan is not agitating against Zia.' There was no real serious challenge to the military. She added that even if he was overthrown, he would be succeeded by another general. However, if the opposition put up a joint front, Zia could be overthrown. At the moment this had to be ruled out.

We also touched on the restlessness in Balochistan. She emphatically denied that her late husband's stand had been anti-Baloch. In fact, he had made Balochistan the fourth state of Pakistan (previously it had been an agency). He had consistently struggled to ensure that divisive elements and feudal lords did not combine to defeat his reforms. She asserted that in a free election, the people of Balochistan would vote for the PPP. She also emphasized that the Pathans of the North West Frontier Province were critical of Zia's Afghan policy.

Up to this point the exchange was politely banal, routine and in real danger of becoming boring. But soon, liveliness took over. I respectfully sought her permission to learn the true facts about her husband's last twenty-four hours. I was doing so with great reluctance. Confusion needed to be cleared; misinformation corrected.

This is what she said. The night before the hanging, the military had raided their home. They were looking for a copy of the Rahman Report which had incriminated the army for brutalities committed in East Pakistan in 1971. They found nothing.

The same night, another group met Chairman Bhutto in jail. They told Bhutto that his life would be spared if he owned responsibility for what happened in East Pakistan instead of the army as mentioned in the report. This he refused to do. Emaciated though he was, he hit out at the offending officer. A scuffle followed. Bhutto fell and his head hit the floor. He died on the spot.

She and her daughters, Benazir and Sanam, had their last meeting with Bhutto late in the evening before the hanging. The chairman had conducted himself with superhuman courage and dignity. The jail superintendent had informed Begum Bhutto that her husband would be hanged at 4.30 a.m. The time was later changed to 2.30 a.m.

The relatives who lowered the body into the grave in Larkana noted that the usual post-hanging features were missing—a swollen tongue, bulging eyes. The neck had not been broken, because the face could be easily turned towards Mecca before the body was interned.

A deep silence followed. I was much moved. All I could say at leaving-taking was, 'Madam, now that we both keep questionable company, I hope contact would be maintained.' She agreed.

The next time I met her was in early 1982, with my wife. Begum Bhutto was quite clearly seriously ill. She insisted that we stay beyond the allotted time. We did. Her gracious hospitality touched us. We spent nearly ninety minutes at her home. She invited me to look at her husband's library. I am a bibliophile and have a ten-thousand book library. Mr Bhutto's library was in a much higher literary sphere. Not one paperback. Autobiographies and biographies filled many shelves. Also history and international affairs.

Begum Bhutto complained that she was not permitted to go abroad for treatment. She was spitting blood, and was not responding to local treatment. I ventured to suggest that if a team of doctors concluded that it was necessary for her to go abroad, they should say so publicly. In that event, appeals could be made on humanitarian grounds to President Zia. The team of doctors obliged. Mrs Gandhi and several other leaders made public appeals. Begum Bhutto was allowed to proceed abroad for treatment. I earned President Zia's chilling wrath.

40

In Russia with Sonia Gandhi and President Putin

Sonia Gandhi arrived in Moscow on the morning of 14 June 2005. I was with her. Deputy Foreign Minister Alexander Grushko received her at the Vnukovo International Airport.

In the afternoon she spoke at the Centre for National Glory, at President Hotel. Her subject was 'Dialogue of Civilizations'. It was a take-off from Samuel Huntington's flawed sermon, 'The Clash of Civilizations'. Our Moscow host Vladimir Yakunin, the chairman of the centre, was also the deputy minister of railways.

In the afternoon, in glorious weather, we left for Vladimir by helicopter. I was at a loss to know why Sonia Gandhi was visiting an obscure medieval town of which I had never heard. On arrival I was struck by the pristine beauty of the place. It was snuggled between tall trees and churches. History had not bypassed Vladimir. Time had. The inhabitants were attired in clothes which had defeated time. No concession to fashion. Sonia and I walked along with our guide. Soon we arrived at an unkempt courtyard. The main building had been a church, now converted into a museum. Inside we came to an octagonal room. On one of the walls were stuck a number of paper slips. Sonia was much interested in these. She reads Russian and was obviously looking for something. 'Natwar, my father was a prisoner of war here during World War II. He escaped, walking all the way to Italy.' She was deeply moved. This was for her a very special moment. I listened. Any comment would have been banal and inappropriate.

The next day we left for St Petersburg, a city of breathtaking beauty and inspiring history, and home to some of Russia's greatest writers including Pushkin and Dostoevsky. A city where in November 1917 Vladimir Lenin had announced the birth of the Soviet Union.

The thousand-day Nazi siege of Leningrad during World War II is an epic saga of defiance and suffering. The city starved but did not yield. It was grievously wounded but emerged with its head held high.

St Petersburg was named after Peter the Great, who called it his 'window on the West'. Its classical colonnades, baroque houses, its impeccable architecture, its splendours will forever remain etched in my mind. It's an alluring city. Its avenues are straight and elegant. The death of communism heralded the renewal of St Petersburg. It is not a parvenu city; it is a reaffirmation of man's ingenuity, a statement of life.

Our host in St Petersburg was President Vladimir Putin. He was staying in the Konstantinovsky Palace overlooking Finland Bay. We were put up in the ducal guest house next to the palace. Putin, unlike his Soviet predecessors, is cultivated, urbane, witty and sophisticated. He has a strong, compact frame. He is a karate champion.

On such occasions Sonia is at her best. Ease of manner stands out. A sagacious listener, she gives nothing away. Her earlier diffidence has given way to self-assurance. I have closely watched the evolution of her personality.

The 'official' talks in the morning lasted ninety minutes and were followed by a working lunch. The menu card I still have. It is signed by Putin, Sonia Gandhi (in Hindi) and myself.

After lunch the president bid goodbye to Sonia Gandhi and wished us a pleasant boat ride on the Gulf of Finland. Sonia and I returned to the guest house to change.

When we arrived at the pier, whom do we see? President Putin waiting to receive Sonia. I told her in a whisper that this was an exceptionally warm and unusual gesture. And it was. Not only that, Putin said he would join us for the forty-minute yacht ride. The affable informality and relaxed ambience was a joy. It was a perfect June day. Blue sky and a shimmering deep blue Finland Bay added enchantment to the outing. The conversation flowed from the jovial to the serious.

At one point I said to the president that Khrushchev was well remembered in India. During his memorable visit to India in 1955 he had, while in Srinagar, on the spur of the moment, announced that Kashmir was a part of India.

Foreign minister Andrei Gromyko was left speechless. His rumbustious boss had made a momentous foreign policy pronouncement without consulting his minister. And that too on so contentious a subject. Khrushchev had become an instant hero in India. Observing how Sonia and I were at so much ease with each other, Putin asked 'Minister, how long have you known Mrs Gandhi's family?' Before I could respond, a smiling Sonia intervened, 'Now, he will go on till the evening.' I told the Russian president that I had known the family since 1944.

A few minutes before we were to disembark, I told Putin how much we had appreciated the overview of developments in Russia by Vladimir Yakunin while in Moscow. On touching ground whom do we see? The ubiquitous Yakunin himself. Putin went up to him and asked, 'What fairy tales have you been telling the foreign minister?' Yakunin's face fell.

We took leave of the president and proceeded to the State Hermitage museum. I had heard much praise of this citadel of art and culture. It had been preserved and treated as a symbol of Russia's rich cultural heritage. I was more than keen to see it. Surely it could not surpass the British and Metropolitan museums of London and New York. Nor could it possibly compare favourably with the Louvre. More importantly, I believed in art for art's sake. The Soviets did not. For them art had to be utilitarian. I was not wholly ignorant of European art. I was more than familiar with Renoir, Gauguin, Cezanne, Monet, Degas.

Sonia's interest, knowledge and understanding of the visual arts was profound. I tagged along with her. She pointed out to me one masterpiece after another. After three hours we walked down to a charming pavilion built by Peter the Great on the shore of the Neva River. It was almost a kilometre's walk. The temperature was over ninety-five degrees. Like her mother-in-law Sonia walks fast. I made no attempt to keep up with her. I thought that after seeing the St Peters Pavilion we would call it a day. No. She said to me, 'Natwar, you are tired. Go back to the guest house. I will spend some more time here.'

After a quiet dinner Vladimir Yakunin took us to 'enjoy' an opera. It was nearly 11 p.m. when the operatic agony ended. I was bleary-eyed. For Sonia it had been a long day. She asked me to tell Yakunin that she would like to return to the guest house. He would have none of it: 'Mrs Gandhi must see the white night over the horizon and that too from a launch.' She relented. I had heard much about the white nights. What I saw was a sight so unique that I shall always remember it. There was no midnight at 12 p.m.—it was a white night. The sky was bathed in a golden glow. The waters were still, so was the sky, and the city.

On the launch Yakunin was sitting opposite me. He walked over in unconcealed excitement. 'Mr Singh, what did you say to the president about me?' I kept a straight face saying that I had told President Putin that 'You are a so and so ...' 'Please don't joke—you are a very important man. The president has appointed me railway minister. I do not know how to thank you.' I said to Sonia that I had made one lifelong friend in Russia.

Next day she left for Delhi. I for Oslo.

41

Margaret Thatcher, Chandraswami and I

India House is among the better-known diplomatic establishments in London. I first set eyes on the imposing building in 1952, when I was a student at Cambridge University. Thirty years later, I entered India House as deputy high commissioner. One of my less attractive duties was to meet the unreasonable demands of visitors from India. Not all were disagreeable but many were.

In the early summer of 1975, Chandraswami telephoned me. He was in London. The late Yashpal Kapoor (of the Emergency fame) had asked him to contact me. Chandraswami invited me to meet him at his place. I said if he wished to see me, he should come to India House. This he did the next day. At the time he was in his late twenties. He was in his 'sadhu' attire. He did not speak a word of English. Now he does.

At this, our first meeting, he dropped names. Well-known names. I was, quite obviously, expected to be impressed. I was not. After a few days, he again came to see me. He invited my wife and me to have dinner with him.

The food was delicious. Chandraswami had already made a few *chelas* who hovered around Swamiji and did his bidding. After dinner he said to us, 'I will show you something you have never seen.' He then produced a large sheet of white paper and drew lines from top to bottom and from left to right, like a chessboard. Next he produced three strips of paper and asked my wife to write a question on each strip, roll it into a ball and then place it on a square on the chessboard. My wife wrote the questions in English. He closed his eyes and went into a trance. I was, by this time, getting restless and looking at my watch. Suddenly, he asked my wife to pick up any one of the paper balls. She did so. And opened it. Chandraswami then told her what the question was. He was spot on. My wife, who is an amateur astrologer, was sceptical at this stage. When Chandraswami got the next two questions right, she was amazed and interested. I was intrigued. Fluke? Not three times. Mind-reading? Maybe. I could not, as a rationalist, accept mumbo-jumbo. Neither could I dismiss Chandraswami as a hoax.

A few days later, Y.B. Chavan, the then external affairs minister, was on his way to the United States. I went to meet him at Heathrow. He confirmed he knew Chandraswami well. 'He does have some kind of *siddhi* (special powers),' the minister said. I also told Chavan that Chandraswami had asked me to arrange a meeting with Lord Mountbatten and also with Mrs Thatcher. Should I arrange these meetings? To my discomfiture and surprise, Chavan saw no harm in Chandraswami meeting either Mountbatten or Margaret

Thatcher. That very evening Chandraswami called me, '*Aagya mil gaee*?'(Got your permission?) By now my unease about Chandraswami was gradually beginning to erode. The fellow had a peculiar charm. He was, in addition, entertaining. Also an accomplished raconteur.

I rang up Lord Mountbatten. He said he would have been glad to meet 'your friend', but could not do so. He was leaving for a holiday in northern Ireland the next day. He would be away for six weeks. I was quite relieved. I informed Chandraswami. What about Mrs Thatcher? Yes, indeed, what about Mrs Thatcher!

She had been elected leader of the Conservative party six months earlier. Doubts still assailed me about Chandraswami meeting Margaret Thatcher, not yet the 'iron lady'. I was taking a risk. Suppose Chandraswami made a fool of himself. I would look the bigger fool.

I sought an appointment with the leader of the Opposition. She promptly obliged. I met her in her tiny office in the House of Commons. I told her, 'I have come on an unusual errand. A young holy man from India is in London. He is a great admirer of yours. He is very keen to meet you and pay his respects.'

Her response was, 'If you think I should meet him, I shall. What does he want to see me for?''That he will tell you himself,' I said. She agreed to meet the holy man, in her House of Commons office, early next week. 'Only ten minutes, Deputy High Commissioner,' she announced. I thanked her and left.

Chandraswami was on cloud nine when I gave him the news. I cautioned him not to do or say anything silly. I was putting my neck on the line for him. '*Chinta mat kariye*' (don't worry), said the sage.

So, to the House of Commons the two of us proceeded. Chandraswami was dressed in his 'sadhu' kit, with a huge tilak on his forehead and a staff in his right hand. *Rudraksha malas* round this neck. He banged the staff on the road till I told him to stop doing so. I confess I had begun to feel self-conscious. Not Chandraswami. Rusticity provides an armour of sorts. Chandraswami is not an unobtrusive individual. He relished the attention he was inviting. Finally we reached Thatcher's office. With her was her parliamentary private secretary, Adam Butler, MP, son of Rab Butler, the Conservative leader.

Introductions over, Mrs Thatcher asked, 'What did you want to see me for?' Chandraswami spoke in Hindi. I translated. 'Tell her she will soon find out.' His tone was arrogantly respectful. Mrs Thatcher said, 'I am waiting.' The clock was ticking away. Chandraswami was in no hurry. He asked for a large piece of paper. He then went through the same routine as with my wife. He gave Thatcher five strips of paper and requested her to write a question on each. She obliged, but with scarcely camouflaged irritation. Chandraswami then asked her to open the first paper ball. She did. He gave the text of the question in Hindi. I translated. Correct. I watched Mrs Thatcher. The irritation gave way to subdued curiosity. Next question. Again bull's eye. Curiosity replaced by interest. By the fourth question the future iron lady's demeanour had changed. She began to look at Chandraswami not as a fraud, but as a holy man indeed.

My body language too had altered. Last question. Correct again. I heaved a sigh of relief. Mrs Thatcher was now perched on the edge of the sofa. Chandraswami was like a triumphant guru. He took off his chappals and sat on the sofa in the lotus pose. I was appalled. Mrs Thatcher seemed to approve. She asked supplementary questions. In each case Chandraswami's response almost overwhelmed the future prime minister. She was on the verge of another question when Chandraswami regally announced that the sun had set. No more questions. I said to Mrs Thatcher that I was only translating word for word. I was in no way responsible for what he said. Thatcher was not put out. She enquired if she could meet him again.

I was entirely unprepared for this. Very coolly, almost condescendingly, he said, 'On Tuesday at 2.30 p.m. at the house of Shri Natwar Singh.' I told him that he was overreaching himself by dictating to Mrs Thatcher the day and time without taking into account her convenience. This was not India. He was unmoved: '*Kunwar sahib, anuvad kar dijiye aur phir dekhiye.*'(Kunwar sahib, translate and then see.) I was astounded when she asked me, 'Deputy High Commissioner, where do you live?'

This was not all. What followed was something out of a weird novel. Just as we were about to leave, Mr Holy Man produced a talisman tied to a not-so-tidy piece of string. He then pronounced that Thatcher should tie it on her left arm when she came to my house on Tuesday. I was now on the verge of losing my temper, something which no diplomat should ever do. I said I will not translate this rubbish. Mrs Thatcher intervened to know what the holy man was saying.

'Mrs Thatcher, please forgive me, but Chandraswami would like you to wear this talisman on your left arm.' She took the talisman. We were saying our goodbyes when Chandraswami produced his sartorial bomb. Turning to me he said, 'Kunwar sahib, kindly tell Mrs Thatcher that on Tuesday she should wear a red *poshak*.' I felt like hitting him. He was overdoing his act. I firmly told him that it was the height of bad manners to tell a lady what she should or should not wear. Thatcher looked a bit apprehensive at this not-so-mild altercation between a distraught deputy high commissioner and a somewhat ill-mannered holy man. Very reluctantly, I said to her that the holy man would be obliged if she wore a red dress on Tuesday. I was looking down at the floor when I said this.

When we got into my car, I told Chandraswami what I thought of his boorish behaviour. He was not one bit perturbed. He was certain she would wear the talisman and the red dress. I also told him that she was being polite and that she would not come to my house on Tuesday. I was wrong.

On Tuesday, at 2.30 p.m. sharp, Margaret Thatcher, leader of the Conservative party, arrived at The Sun House, 9, Frognal Way, Hampstead. It was a beautiful day. She was wearing a splendid red dress. The talisman too was in its proper place.

She asked many questions but the most important related to the chances of her becoming prime minister. My wife was also present. Chandraswami did not disappoint Thatcher. He prophesied that she would be prime minister for nine, eleven or thirteen years. Thatcher, no doubt, believed that she would be PM one day. But nine, eleven or thirteen years seemed a bit much. I and my wife thought the same too. Thatcher put one final question. When would she become the prime minister? Chandraswami pronounced: in three or four years. He was proved right. She was PM for eleven years.

This narrative should have ended here. But there was an aftermath. The Commonwealth summit was held in Lusaka, Zambia, in 1979.Margaret Thatcher had by then become the prime minister of the United Kingdom. I had been posted to Zambia in August 1977. Along with other high commissioners I went to the Lusaka airport to receive Thatcher. When she greeted me and my wife, I gently whispered, 'Our man has been proved right.' For a moment she looked flustered. Then she took me aside, 'High Commissioner, we don't talk about these matters.' 'Of course not, Prime Minister, of course not,' said I.

42
The Ubiquitous Swami

I have already related the Margaret Thatcher–Chandraswami encounter. Now I will relate two more uncanny incidents. One in 1985; the other in 1989.

Commonwealth summits are held every two years. The 1985 summit was scheduled for September at Nassau, the capital of the Bahamas. I was at the time minister of state for fertilizers, a ministry as far from foreign affairs as the North Pole is from the equator. Regardless, Prime Minister Rajiv Gandhi involved me in the preparations under way for the summit. I took a reconnaissance jaunt to the capital of the host country. Could a tiny island manage so colossal an undertaking?

I arrived at New York in early September on my way to Nassau. We had no resident mission in the Bahamas. Our ambassador in Washington was concurrently accredited to the island state. I asked the permanent representative of India to the UN to get in touch with his counterpart in Nassau to arrange my meeting with Prime Minister Lynden Pindling.

I waited a couple of days. There was no response from the permanent mission of the Bahamas. It had been a frustrating wait. I decided to proceed to Washington to try my luck there. Ambassador Pratap Kaul contacted the ambassador of the Bahamas and requested him to arrange my meeting with his PM for discussing the agenda of the summit and also look at the *bandobast* (arrangements). The 1983 summit had met in New Delhi. As its chief coordinater, I had acquired a thoroughly undeserved reputation as a bandobast expert. In Washington, too, we fared no better than in New York. Obviously, the embassies of the Bahamas were a recusant tribe. After three wasted days I decided to return to New York. It had been an annoying wild goose chase. Then fate intervened. The ambassador informed me that Chandraswami wished to speak to me. I was both intrigued and surprised. How in the name of heaven did the swami get to know of my presence in Washington DC?

Pratap Kaul informed me that Chandraswami was in Ottawa. When I spoke to him he was chuckling away: '*Kunwar sahib, Pindling se meeting nahin ho rahi hain aapki.*' (Kunwar sahib, you are unable to have a meeting with Pindling.) 'How do you know?' I asked, somewhat annoyed by his one-upmanship. He ignored my question and announced, '*Main aap ki meeting ka intizam kar diya hai. Pindling aap se kal milega.*' (I have arranged for a meeting. Pindling will meet you tomorrow.) I am seldom at a loss for words. This, however, was astounding. Where our missions in New York and Washington had not succeeded, Chandraswami had! He had pulled off a minor diplomatic coup. Puzzled, I asked, 'How did you know that I was in Washington?' '*Kunwar sahib, main aap ki khabar rakhta hoon.*' (Kunwar sahib, I keep track of you.) This was even more mystifying, because I had not had any contact with him for many years. His networking skills were impressive indeed.

I did get to see the prime minister in Nassau. Sun, sand, sea and surf made it a paradise for burning the candle at both ends and in the middle too. Authors were writing their masterpieces in seaside cottages. The uninhibited—they were in a vast majority—were full of bounce and bohemianism and much else.

This was Rajiv Gandhi's first summit. He excelled. He spoke after Margaret Thatcher and performed brilliantly. He was the youngest of the heads. He was not hesitant or intimidated. Several leaders walked over to congratulate him after his speech. I distinctly remember the Sri Lankan president J.R. Jayewardene and the prime minister of Singapore, Lee Kuan Yew, among others.

This was a special gesture. Rajiv Gandhi was pleased and surprised. After all, he was a novice fallen among ageing heavyweight political dinosaurs.

An aside that I recall fondly. During the summit a cricket match between India and Sri Lanka was on. I asked Rajiv to send Jayewardene this note: 'I wish Sri Lanka luck and India success.' Jayewardene replied, 'Thanks. I wish India luck and Sri Lanka success.'

Four years passed. I was in Paris, leading the Indian delegation to the conference on 'Banning of Chemical Weapons.' On the second day I came down with flu. My throat was so sore I felt as if razor blades were cutting against my tonsils. I felt miserable and irritated. My speech had to be postponed. My private secretary was showing me a few coded telegrams when the telephone rang. 'Sir, Mr Chandraswami is on the line.' It was far too uncanny. But true. I was in no mood to talk but could not resist speaking to the wandering swami. 'Kunwar sahib, you are not feeling well. Who is looking after you?' I said, 'First tell me, how did you come to know of my illness and presence in Paris?' 'I will tell you when I meet you. I am bringing President Mitterrand's doctor to see you.' 'How do you know the president's doctor?' "This too I will tell you when we meet.' Within half an hour he arrived with the doctor. The doctor examined me and wrote out a prescription. I was getting more and more curious. I asked the doctor, 'How do you know Mr Chandraswami?' He answered, 'He is my guru.'

Chandraswami was grinning from ear to ear. He was in his sadhu garments. After a few minutes the doctor left.

Chandraswami was in his element. 'I am flying tomorrow to Belgrade to meet the president of Yugoslavia. He is sending his private plane to pick me up.' This I thought was going over the top. 'Any more fairy tales?' I asked. Just then the telephone rang. My personal secretary said, 'Sir, our ambassador in Belgrade is on the line.' I was dumbfounded. The ambassador informed me that 'Mr Chandraswami would be arriving in Belgrade tomorrow in the president's personal plane. Should I receive him at the airport?' The swamiji was grinning. I gave the ambassador a masterly diplomatic answer, 'Use your judgement.'

43

A Medium Called Albert Best

Albert Best was a most remarkable Irishman, who during his life brought solace and comfort to thousands of grieving people. Himself from the working class, he influenced people of all kinds, cutting across religion, class, creed and even reaching out to non-believers. He was a bridge between this life and the world of spirits.

Albert Best was born in Belfast on 2 December 1917. He was perhaps among the greatest mediums of his generation. During World War II he served as a soldier in North Africa. He was severely wounded and left for burial with eight other corpses. A voice told him to 'get up', which he did, and walked away. He was again wounded, captured and tortured in a German camp. He was invalided and sent back to England in a ship. On arrival he was told that his wife and three children had been killed in a bombing raid in Belfast. Albert wondered why he had not received any letters from his wife. He was told the mails weren't getting through.

In 1944 he began attending the Kilmarnock Spiritualist Church. It soon became evident that Albert's extrasensory perceptions enabled him to communicate with spirits in the other world. Like the Hindus he believed that the body perishes, but the soul is immortal.

My wife met Albert in early 1970 in England through another medium. She believes that a highly evolved medium like Albert can help us establish contact with people who have passed on. Time and time again through Albert she has been able to communicate with her father, who died in 1974, and many others. Later with our daughter who left us in 2002. This was through a young medium friend of Albert's whom he had introduced to Heminder.

What is the definition of a medium? A medium is the instrument who has the ability to connect a person from this world with someone from the other world. As the years passed, Albert's name and fame spread. He became known beyond the British Isles. He was invited to the US, South Africa, Australia and New Zealand. In each country he provided 'living' proof that mediums possessed something that most people did not.

Albert Best came to India four times in the 1980s and '90s, as our guest. By word of mouth the news of his being in Delhi spread. With each visit the number of seekers multiplied. They were in need of consolation and solace. They came from all walks of life. No one left disappointed. Besides being a medium, he was also an accomplished healer.

The reader might rightly ask, 'This is too vague and amorphous. Can you be more precise?' I shall give only two concrete examples while explaining the methodology first.

His practice was to make a person sit on a chair opposite him, and then sometimes he would go into a trance. The 'sitting' had begun. He would say to him or her, 'Your "X", whom you have lost, is here and asks you to look for the watch you are missing in the third drawer of your study table under some papers.' It was indeed found there. The point was to prove that there indeed was communication with loved ones.

Aslam and Feroza Khan are good friends of ours. Aslam is well known in the sports world. He was for a short while a minister in Uttar Pradesh. Feroza is a fine painter. Their son, Afzal, was my son Jagat's closest friend at Doon School. During holidays he often stayed with us in our home—9, Safdarjung Road. He was a born charmer. Handsome, loving, ebullient and amusing. He became a part of the family. The 1989 UP elections had been called. Afzal left Delhi for Dehradun to be with his parents. His father was a candidate. He decided to follow the jeep carrying some of the sealed ballot boxes so that these would not be tampered with. His vehicle was stopped by armed thugs. Afzal protested. He was shot and died on the spot. He was only twenty years old. His parents were shattered. We were devastated.

Some months later, Aslam and Feroza had a sitting with Albert at our home. His death had completely destroyed the symmetry of their lives. Their sorrow was deep and all-pervasive. On their way from Dehradun to our place they were delayed by traffic. My wife observed that Albert was restless. He kept saying, 'Afzal is already here and is keen to "talk" to his parents.' The parents 'met' Afzal who told them what had happened on the day of his death. He did not see the weapon with which he was shot as it was hidden under the shirt of the assailant. This sitting lasted several sessions. With every session the sorrow of the parents receded and serenity took over.

Albert Best went into coma on 2 April 1996. On 11 April 1996 he came out of his coma, looked at the foot of his hospital bed and said to his three friends who were present, 'Don't hold me back. My family has come to take me.'

On 12 April he 'drifted out of the harbour on a silent tide.'

PS: Readers might be interested to learn that R.K. Narayan, the author of the Malgudi novels, remained in almost daily contact with his wife, who died aged thirty in 1940. R.K. lived to be ninety-six. His novel *The English Teacher* is largely about this dimension of his life.

44

An Encounter with Qi Baishi

Qi Baishi (Chi Pai-Shih) will rank among the top twenty artists of all time. His paintings (not one in oil) sold for Rs 1,505 crores in 2010. I am probably the only Indian who met the distinguished and venerable Qi Baishi. Peking (not yet Beijing), in the mid-1950s, had three towering figures from the refined worlds of painting, dance and literature. The dance maestro was Mei Lanfang, a friend and contemporary of Uday Shankar. They had first met in New York in 1931. Mei Lanfang was the greatest Peking opera dancer of all time. Even in his late fifties he continued to play female roles. On several occasions he gave me tickets to watch him perform. During the Japanese occupation he grew a moustache and successfully evaded the invaders.

Lao She was the literary giant. He had lived many years in the United States. In 1949 PM Chou En-Lai invited him to come home, which Lao She did. His novel *Rickshaw Boy* was a world bestseller. I met him two or three times, once in the company of Han Suyin, the author of *A Many-Splendoured Thing*. Lao She committed suicide during the Cultural Revolution.

I had seen the brush paintings of Chi Pai-Shih in many offices and museums. He mostly painted birds, shrimps, crickets, chickens. He patiently studied their activities before painting them. During the war, 1941–45, Chi became popular with American soldiers. They were no connoisseurs of art but were attracted by the celebrity status of Chi. He would sell a painting of a chicken for ten dollars. The Yankee would howl, 'Master Chi, two chickens for ten dollars. Please draw one more.' This Chi did. He did not begin life as a painter. For years he was a carpenter (similar to M.F. Husain, who at one time made wooden toys). His date of birth is somewhat flexible. It is generally agreed that Chi was born in 1863 in Hunan province.

Getting to see him was an occasion in itself. The Chinese vice-minister of culture, Chen Chen Tho, was good enough to help arrange the pilgrimage. I had got to know the minister in 1954 when he led a cultural delegation to India. Chen was a scholar of repute and an expert on Rabindranath Tagore. He died in an air crash a few years later.

For several years after the founding of the People's Republic of China in 1949, the government paid no attention to Chi. Then a dramatic event occurred. Prime Minister Chou En-Lai called on him on his ninetieth birthday in January 1953. Life changed overnight. Master-artist Chi was allotted a house, provided with a servant. Occasionally he was exhibited to foreign dignitaries. He became a national icon. His paintings were suddenly in demand.

I arrived at his house on 17 December 1956 at 11 a.m. It was bitterly cold. I was greeted by a smartly dressed (in blue Mao outfit) young man. I walked across a modest courtyard to reach his sanctum–study. For a brief moment I did not notice him. His tiny frame was crumpled on a comfortable chair. He was wearing a black cap and was dressed in the pre-1949 long cotton overcoat (no buttons) which was wrapped round him. The sun shone through the window above his head. I was hell-bent on getting as much out of the visit as possible.

At first he did not register my presence. I asked a question or two. His son (the young man who had received me) shouted in his father's ear. For a second or two the eyes lost their opacity, the mind connected but the body did not cooperate and he sank back into the chair. Then suddenly he came to and offered me piping hot green tea. I enquired who his favourite Chinese painter was. 'Chen Pan Ting'. The name meant nothing to me. I was expecting him to name Hsu Pei-Hung, famous for his painting of horses. Next question. 'Have you seen any Indian paintings?' 'Yes, I have seen Indonesian paintings,' came the reply. At ninety-three, India and Indonesia were one and the same! Then I asked, 'What do you think of the Peace Prize you received?' 'I don't know if my paintings have any peaceful content.'

He had never been out of China. He told me he no longer painted. He used to paint directly with a brush, on Chinese paper. No pencil drawing. I learnt he was also an expert in seal engravings on ivory. In his youth he wrote poetry.

I bought two of his paintings. The son was a bit of a wheeler dealer and sold fake works. Mine were not. I paid the equivalent of Rs 600 for them. One with four chickens and an exquisite one of a black eagle, twenty-four feet long.

When I left, Chi Pai-Shih got up to shake hands and walked to the door to see me off. This is how I remember him—waving like a little angel.

45

The Dalai Lama Arrives in India

The day His Holiness the Dalai Lama crossed the Tibet–India border in the closing hours of March 1959, I was in Prime Minister Jawaharlal Nehru's office in South Block with the IFS probationers of the 1958 batch. After 1957 the PM did not meet new entrants to the IFS individually but received the entire batch. I was taking down notes. The PM asked me, '*Kya likh rahe ho*?' (What are you writing?) Before I could answer, Foreign Secretary S. Dutt walked in and whispered in the PM's right ear. Almost immediately the PM got up saying that he had to be in Parliament as something of great significance had cropped up. Later we learnt that the Dalai Lama had sought asylum in India. Nehru immediately responded positively. This was in keeping with our age-old tradition of offering hospitality.

The reaction in China was ferociously vituperative: 'The reactionaries in India have always harboured expansionist ambitions towards Tibet and have carried out various forms of sabotage activities.' The Dalai Lama was dubbed 'a rebel'.

The *People's Daily* of Peking wrote: 'We give a solemn warning to imperialists and Indian expansionists: you must stop at once; otherwise you will be crushed to pieces under iron fists of 650 million Chinese people.' Hardly the language of a friendly country committed to the principles of the Panchsheel Treaty (signed between India and China in 1954).

Although the government had firmly told His Holiness to refrain from making controversial pronouncements, he did make statements which could have been avoided. His taking the Tibet question to the UN in September 1959 was ill-advised. He did so contrary to the advice of the Indian government.

His Holiness has now been in India for fifty-three years. Some time back he announced his decision to give up his secular duties and concentrate on his spiritual activities. The announcement caused consternation among his devotees and followers. China reacted in a churlish and peevish manner. I have been following events in China for more than five decades. To me it is incomprehensible how a great country (which was Buddhist till 1949) can be so afraid of and obsessed with a man who is respected, revered and venerated by millions of people all over the globe. He preaches compassion, forgiveness, goodness, magnanimity and life-enhancing precepts of Buddhism. His personality is so engaging that he casts a spell on anyone who meets him. Inner light radiates from him.

On arrival in India, the Dalai Lama spent a few days in Tezpur, then proceeded to Mussoorie, where Nehru had prolonged talks with him. He came down to Delhi in September and was put up at Hyderabad House. I was attached as temporary liaison officer to His Holiness. He met very many people including the upcoming poet Dom Moraes. The Dalai Lama was in a playful mood. Dom referred to nature helping him during his escape from Lhasa—blinding storms, thunder, lightning, etc. His Holiness replied that nothing unusual happened. Such weather was usual in Tibet during that time of the year. This somewhat deflated Dom.

The Dalai Lama called on several cabinet ministers. All treated him with respect in spite of his age—twenty-four only. His meeting with Home Minister Govind Ballabh Pant I remember vividly. We were ushered into a small room which, if I remember, was used as a reception room for receiving the distinguished and the eminent. The Dalai Lama sat opposite Pandit Pant. His interpreter next to him. Raja Pant, Govind Pant's son, was also present. I occupied a chair behind His Holiness. Top-secret matters were being discussed with complete candour. Half-way through the meeting Pantji looked at me and asked, 'Who are you?' I was taken aback. Relief came when the home minister next pointed to a man sitting behind me, who nervously said he was from the Press Trust of India. The Dalai Lama was startled. After all, he and the home minister were dealing with diplomatic dynamite. I had no doubt in my mind that Pantji would ask the more-than-errant PTI eavesdropper to leave the room. This he did not. Instead he requested the

Dalai Lama to continue. I thought the minister's decision strange. After the close of the meeting, Pantji asked the man to stay behind. He then proceeded to read out the Riot Act to him. If a single word of what was discussed became known, the consequences for him would be most unpleasant. Nothing was ever published.

What mystified me at first was Pantji letting the man stay. I later understood. Had the PTI man been sent out, he would have reached for the nearest phone and filed a story. That would have caused serious complications. To this day I have not forgotten Pantji's serenity, sagacity and masterly handling of a tricky situation. He was among the greatest of our home ministers.

46

A Brief Rendezvous with Don Bradman

My three non-Indian twentieth-century heroes are Don Bradman, General Vo Nguyen Giap and Nelson Mandela. I have met General Giap and Mr Mandela several times. Sir Donald Bradman only once.

In October 1989 I carried letters from Prime Minister Rajiv Gandhi to Prime Minister David Lange of New Zealand and Prime Minister Bob Hawke of Australia. David Lange was the wittiest man I have ever met. The meeting with him was cordial and relaxed. The one with Bob Hawke did not go so well. His accent was haute Australian.

Hawke backed a predecessor of his—Malcolm Fraser—for the post of secretary general of the Commonwealth. We did not. Hawke, if memory serves me right, took it for granted that Fraser would make it. Rajiv Gandhi and Bob got on well. Both were severely critical of Margaret Thatcher's policy on South Africa. Indira Gandhi thought poorly of Bob Hawke at the 1983 Commonwealth Heads of Government Meeting held in Delhi in November. This was Hawke's first summit. He was not familiar with the subtle nuances of international diplomacy. The Indian PM practised benign neglect of the not-so-charming Australian. (Margaret Thatcher was a bully and generally got her way. Not with Indira Gandhi.)

Now back to Prime Minister Bob Hawke. I gave him Rajiv Gandhi's letter which he kept on a table by his side without reading. Fair enough. Then he came to Malcolm Fraser's candidature. He said Commonwealth countries were showing 'intellectual lethargy' and delaying their decision on the secretary general's election. And more of the same. Ministers of state are at a disadvantage when parleying with prime ministers. At the same time, it was impossible to let a high-handed PM get away without being challenged. I said that India was not intellectually lethargic. The fact was Malcolm Fraser did not have enough support. India supported Sonny Ramphal who was doing a splendid job. Hawke calmed down and the meeting did not end on a discordant note.

Soon after I learnt that later in the evening Hawke was flying to Sydney for a dinner with Don Bradman. I sent Joint Secretary A.K. Budhiraja, who was accompanying me, to find out if I could possibly take a lift to Sydney. The previous day I had driven from Canberra to Sydney, for the Australian airlines were on strike. Had my meeting with the PM ended on a discordant note, I would not have asked this favour.

On the flight Hawke was both charming and friendly. He was in a dinner jacket and a black tie and reading from a folder. It was his speech for the Bradman dinner. Swallowing my pride, I was about to ask if I could meet Bradman. But before I could do so, Hawke came up with a verbal gem. 'Minister, would you like to join the Bradman dinner?' All my life I had dreamt of meeting the great Don. As a school boy I had even written him a fan letter. I kept a scrapbook full of his pictures.

I thanked Hawke saying that I was not properly dressed, but I would very much like to meet Sir Don Bradman who was one of my heroes. 'Of course, Minister.' It would be foolish of me to say that I was not excited. I was.

We arrived at the hotel. We were taken to the prime ministerial room. Sir Donald and Lady Bradman were already there. So was Sir Colin Cowdrey. My eyes were glued to my hero, all of 5' 7". Dinner jacket, balding, eighty-one years of age. 'Don, this is Minister Singh from India,' said Bob Hawke. My pulse quickened. This did not happen to me even when I had met Fidel Castro. I put my hand out and so did Sir Don. Silence. Then the great man spoke: 'Not too long ago I met your railways minister, I forget his name. Nice chap.' He was referring to Madhavrao Scindia. 'Sir Donald, I have been hero-worshipping you since my school days. I am deeply honoured and moved to meet you,' I said. How many times must have Bradman heard such inane remarks. A photographer appeared. After some hesitation I asked Sir Don if I could have a photograph with him. 'Why not?' said Hawke. The photo was taken. The PM, the Bradmans, Sir Colin and myself. Next day the photo was published in the newspapers. I had been cut out.

47
Nehru and Gordimer

Among the whites who opposed apartheid, two names stand out: Alan Paton, the author of *Cry, the Beloved Country*, and Nadine Gordimer, who was awarded the Nobel Prize for Literature in 1991.

I first heard of Gordimer (born 1923) when I was high commissioner to Zambia in the late 1970s. Both she and Paton were relentlessly condemned and harassed by the racists. Neither bent nor bowed.

In early 1991 I, as vice-chairman of the Indira Gandhi Memorial Trust, was asked by Sonia Gandhi to invite Nadine Gordimer to the fourth Indira Gandhi International Conference to be held in New Delhi in November. She accepted. On 13 October she was awarded the Nobel Prize for Literature. I sent her my congratulations. She thanked me and also expressed her inability to come to India in November as she would now have to change her schedule for the next few months. She was distressed 'at having let you down. I hope you will forgive me for this dereliction, and that I may be able to visit India under your auspices at some later date.'

Two years later, the Jawaharlal Nehru Memorial Fund invited her to deliver the 1995 Nehru Memorial Lecture on 13 November, a day before Nehru's birthday. The subject of her lecture was 'Our Century'. She touched our hearts and stirred our minds. It was literature on a grand scale. She commanded our attention as no other Nehru Memorial lecturer had in recent years. She was candid. Her mind was richly endowed. She was provocative, speaking up for socialism with a human face. On Nehru, Gandhi and Mandela she was superb. She spoke of breaking colour and creed barriers. While concluding she quoted Nehru, who in prison had written about 'the problems of individual and social life, of harmonious living, of a proper balancing of an individual's inner and outer life, of an adjustment of the relations between individuals and groups, of a continuous becoming something better and higher, of social development, of the ceaseless adventure of man'.

During her four days in New Delhi, I was lucky to have several informal, spontaneous conversations with the diminutive and still beautiful Nobel laureate. These were not interviews. At a dinner at my home she was at ease, relaxed and disarmingly reflective. Sonia Gandhi was also present.

N.S.: Were you surprised to receive the Nobel?

N.G.: Yes, I was. Mind you, I had been shortlisted but had never really thought I would get it.

N.S.: How did you hear the news?

N.G.: I was in New York, got a telephone call from a friend in London.

N.S.: Has it changed your life?

N.G.: No. At the same time, the demands on my time have increased. Vast correspondence. Invitations. I have learnt to say 'No'. The other side is that you can give a push here and there for a cause or something. Attention is paid. The prestige of the prize helps.

We talked of Attenborough's film *Gandhi*. Also of Forster's *A Passage to India*. Not surprisingly, the conversation drifted to David Lean's film adaptation of the book. I said I had strong views about Lean's production. It was an outrage. In his lifetime Forster had turned down all suggestions of his novels being filmed. Once writer Santha Rama Rau suggested to him to allow her and me to write a film script for *A Passage to India*. Forster replied, 'No.' He told me. 'I would not be able to control the production.' Nadine Gordimer wondered why Satyajit Ray did not do it.

Another day we debated the merits of Nelson Mandela's autobiography *Long Walk to Freedom*. She said, 'The first half was written by Nelson Mandela in Robben Island and smuggled out. It is so good. The second half is done by Richard Stengel. So the book suffers. At one stage Anthony Sampson was to collaborate with Mandela, but somehow it did not unfortunately work out.' At that time my enthusiasm for *Long Walk to Freedom* precluded even the mildest criticism. My hero worship of Mandela was undiluted. When I re-read the book a decade later, I came to the same conclusion as Nadine Gordimer.

N.S.: What are your impressions of Ajanta and Ellora? You have just been there.

N.G.: The history of art and architecture is so Eurocentric.

The Sistine Chapel appears small compared to the great art I saw at Ajanta and Ellora. And so much older.

N.S.: How did you get interested in India?

N.G.: When I was a young girl, I came across Stella Kramrisch's book on Indian art, was fascinated by it and had wished to see Ajanta and Ellora ever since. The setting of the caves is wonderful.

It was a rare opportunity to hear her overview of the current situation in her country. I asked how the land problem was being tackled. Eighty per cent of the land was owned by whites.

N.S.: Would they part with it without a fight?

N.G.: Yes, this is a serious problem but the government is working out an acceptable formula. In many cases the government would buy the land and give it to the blacks.

N.S.: The post-Mandela scenario. How do you see that?

N.G.: He is, of course, the greatest man in the world. There are excellent people with him. They will take over. The bureaucracy is a problem.

N.S.: What about Chief Buthelezi?

N.G.: He is a negative element—always walking out of cabinet meetings.

N.S.: The Indian community—its future?

N.G.: They were a part of the struggle against apartheid and suffered much. The speaker is now an Indian. Ahmed Kathrada, who was with Mandela in Robben Island, is in charge of the president's office. The Indian community should have no fears.

On the day she was leaving, I took advantage of her kindness and pestered her with a couple of more questions.

N.S.: When did you first hear of Gandhi?

N.G.: I came across his book *Satyagraha in South Africa* when I was seventeen or eighteen, and I was deeply affected.

N.S.: And Forster?

N.G.: I must have been ten or eleven when I read *A Passage to India* and thought it a wonderful book. Still do.

I am indebted to her in more ways than one, and treasure the inscribed copy of her book *Writing and Being*. She wrote: 'It was a pleasure to meet as like minds.'

48

Husain the Genius

In early 1957 Maqbool Fida Husain held an exhibition of his paintings at the All India Fine Arts and Crafts Society gallery, New Delhi. Dr Zakir Hussain, the vice-chancellor of the Aligarh Muslim University, arrived unannounced. Walking up to Husain he said, '*Khaqsar ko bhi Hussain kehte hain.*' (This humble man is also known by the name of Hussain.) What a marvellous episode!

I first met M.F. Husain in the summer of 1958, at the Wellesley Road (now Zakir Hussain Marg) flat of Narayan Menon, deputy director general, All India Radio. I asked Han Suyin, the author of *A Many-Splendoured Thing*, to come along. There he was, the future genius—tall, thin, black-bearded, vaguely resembling an Old Testament prophet. He had not yet 'arrived' but was well on the way to becoming the most talented, most sought after Indian painter of world renown. We soon became friends. He was great fun to be with. Among his endearing quirks was to be chronically unpunctual. He was a genius to whom mundane standards could not apply, and never did. He set the pace of his life, not the clock.

In early 1961 I bought a Fiat car (for Rs 11,000). I was then living in the Delhi Gymkhana Club. Husain dropped in to ask if he could borrow my car for a couple of hours. 'Yes, but drive carefully. It's brand new.' '*Barkhurdar, fiqar mat karo*' (do not worry), and off he went. He turned up two days later. For forty-eight hours I was on tenterhooks. I was livid. More worried about my car than Husain. I knew he had no driving licence. I asked, 'Where the hell have you been?' 'Kanpur' was the brief reply. It sounds funny today, but I was not amused then. To make up for it, he painted an enchanting portrait of my companion, a very beautiful young lady. That painting is fifty years old.

While I was living in New York between 1961 and 1966, Husain stayed with me twice. My apartment became a studio of sorts. He painted portraits of R.K. Narayan, Ved Mehta, Pearl Buck, and two of mine.

One morning he announced, 'I am leaving this evening.' I asked where he was leaving for. The answer, 'I will decide when I get to the airport.'

Years went by. I returned to India in early 1966. I was selected to serve in Prime Minister Indira Gandhi's secretariat. Husain and I met often. He took me to a kebab shop in old Delhi many times. He lived in a room in Jangpura. He had no telephone. I used my PM secretariat perch to get him one.

From time to time he expressed a wish to do a portrait of Indira Gandhi. I spoke to the PM. 'No formal sitting, Natwar,' she said. I conveyed this to Husain. A Saturday in early January 1970 was fixed. To my great relief and surprise he arrived five minutes before time. With a chuckle he said, '*Zara ghadi dekho.*' (Just look at your watch.)

I ushered him into the PM's room in her South Block office. After depositing him in a chair opposite the PM I made a move to leave. 'Natwar, sit down, otherwise I will become self-conscious.' I obeyed. As was her habit she kept looking at the files on her desk. Husain got down to work without any ceremony. In a few minutes he was done. He gave the sketch to the PM. She looked at it for half a minute. 'You have made the lower half of my face resemble my father's.' Husain took the sketch back and started all over again. The second effort was approved.

While coming out of the PM's room I said to him, let me tell you that to fit you in, appointments of several visiting ministers had to be rescheduled. He was not impressed. '*Accha kiya. Khurafat bakte.*' (Good. They would have spoken rubbish.)

When he stayed with us in London in 1974 or so, he had achieved iconic status. His fortunes had changed. Not his character. He remained austere, non-pompous, lived on air, walked barefoot, held a long brush, travelled without baggage, with only a *thela*. His paintings were selling. Our children adored him. He was great fun, but never flippant.

Husain was a very great artist. He was also a great human being. He was born with not even a copper spoon in his mouth. He never went to any university. He was endowed with a self-awareness no university could give. Life and love, art and friends, passion and paint were his priorities. He knew his worth and was grateful for it. He distrusted the establishment and never got onto any bandwagon. Sharada

Prasad and I persuaded him to accept a nomination to the Rajya Sabha in 1986. He did so with grace. His *Sansad Nama* is an extraordinary work. I still remember his absent-mindedly walking into the Lok Sabha. A staggering parliamentary folly, but he got away with it. Artistic licence—yes, that's the phrase.

He lived a long life. A good life. He was a very wealthy man towards the latter part of his life. He once told me, 'I know the importance of money, but I have no love for it.' Husain was not just a great artist. He was a phenomenon. He had a presence. I last met him in 2005. I got news of him from mutual friends when he shifted to Dubai and Qatar. Freshness and buoyancy never deserted him. The wounds bigots inflicted on him affected him deeply. He wanted to return to his homeland to die. That was not to be. This star of high voltage leaves behind an army of friends, admirers, devotees and chelas who will always miss him.

49

All's Well That Ends Well

One of the most joyful experiences of my life was my friendship with two wonderful and gifted human beings. In every way both were exceptional. Sunil and Nargis Dutt opened many doors and enriched my life.

Sunil bhai was for thirty years one of my closest friends. He was a first-rate film actor. More importantly, he was a great human being. Large-hearted, compassionate, public-spirited and sensitive. His wife was not only the most beautiful woman of her generation, she was also the queen of post-1947 cinema.

I first met Mrs Nargis Dutt in the most bizarre circumstances in the summer of 1976 in London. I was at the time deputy high commissioner there. Between May and September a large number of Indians arrived in the British capital. Many of them came to shop. Among their most frequented destinations was Marks and Spencer in Oxford Street. Nargis was no exception.

One sultry July afternoon I was in my office in India House when I received a telephone call from the manager of Air India. He gave me the startling news that the film star Nargis was with him. She was sobbing and in acute anxiety. The police had picked her up as she walked out of Marks and Spencer and charged her for shoplifting. She was discharged after 'confessing' and told to appear in court the next morning. She now wanted to come to India House to seek help. I instructed the manager to send her to my office. I also asked my wife to join me.

Nargis Dutt arrived—drained, dishevelled and in tears. We told her to calm down and tell us her tale of woe. This is what she said. She had bought some hosiery items, and paid for them. She then remembered that she had forgotten to buy some more clothes. She absent-mindedly forgot to pay and walked out. She was immediately caught by the police and taken to the police station. She pleaded innocence. She was not believed. Confused and shocked she 'confessed'. Having heard her I said, 'Since you have already "confessed", the matter ends there. Why did you do so if you were innocent?' Her answer was, 'I was so frightened of going to jail, so in panic I "confessed".'

I had an appointment at the Foreign Office which could not be postponed. I asked Hem, my wife, to keep Mrs Dutt company. On the way to the Foreign Office I asked myself why should Nargis shoplift. She was famous, wealthy. She was a charismatic and iconic individual. It made no sense. My instinct told me she was innocent. In any case it was my duty to assist Indians whenever the necessity arose. I decided I would stand by her. After my official business was over, I asked Mr P if I could bring up a delicate and pressing matter with him. 'Go ahead,' he said.

I related the melancholy tale. The Indian counterpart of Elizabeth Taylor was in my office, frightened and sobbing. If the newspapers got hold of the story, it would become another irritant in Indo-British relations. As it is the Emergency had soured them. Besides, no one in India would believe that their leading cine heroine had committed petty larceny. P heard me out. His response was: 'Since she has "confessed" what can we do?' 'Help,' I said. It is no secret that the British establishment is good at benign news management. Could he, I implored, be so good as to ensure that the incident was not unduly played up by the media. I realized I had no authority to ask for such a favour. I took the risk because I was convinced that Nargis was not a kleptomaniac.

P left me and returned after a few minutes. He asked me, 'What is her name on the passport?' I had no idea. Using his telephone I called Nargis. She enlightened me. The name on the passport was Fatima. He noted it. He frankly said he could give no assurance but would see 'if we can do something informally'. The good man suggested that it would be wise for Nargis to go to the court the next day in plain clothes and wear dark glasses.

I thanked him and returned to India House. Sitting in my private secretary's office was the London correspondent of *The Indian Express*. He gave me a copy of the story he intended to file. His story did not appear.

Next morning, plain Miss Fatima went to the court, paid the fine and was let off. The British press ignored the incident. This would never have happened without the 'back channel' assistance of P.

On her return to India, she wrote me a letter on 10 July

1976. '... I don't find words to thank you for all that you did for me. If not for your efforts, I would have been crucified by my own people. Instead of facing humiliation, I would have killed myself. I owe my life and prestige to you. I am indebted to you for life. I will go and see Mrs Gandhi and try to explain to her exactly as things happened ...'

Five years later, she lost her life to cancer. She was only fifty-two. She lived a short life with glory.

50

Remembering Dev Anand

I do not claim intimacy but I knew the late Dev Anand since our first meeting at the UN in New York in 1962. It was summer. Somehow he traced me out. He needed no introduction. I did. He had learnt that I knew the novelist R.K. Narayan well. Could I give him a letter of introduction? I said I would be glad to do so, but could he tell me why he wished me to do so. He said he wanted Narayan's permission to make a film of his novel *The Guide*. I obliged. A few days later, Narayan wrote back: 'It was awfully good of you to give my address to Dev Anand who wrote to me and then met me and we have arrived at a very satisfactory arrangement for the production of *The Guide*, both in Hindi and English.'

Years rolled by. In October 1969 Dev Anand came to Delhi and sought me out. I was then working at Indira Gandhi's office. Dev Anand said he was keen that the prime minister watch his latest film *Prem Pujari*. Could I arrange for him to meet her and invite her? I spoke to the PM. She agreed. Word got around that the PM would be receiving Dev Anand at her

South Block office. Work almost stopped in the Ministry of External Affairs. The corridors were soon teeming with the hierarchy waiting to see Dev Anand. From lower division assistants to IFS officers, all crowded the corridors. I took Dev in. He requested the PM to see his film. She said she would like to do so but was very preoccupied. However she would try to adjust her schedule. At the end of the meeting, she walked down the corridor with Dev Anand and myself. By now the bureaucracy was out in every nook and corner to see the rare sight of Indira Gandhi and the matinee idol walking together. Before getting into her car she asked me to see the film and let her know what I thought of it.

Dev took me to the cinema hall of the Air Force establishment on Safdarjung Road. I liked the film and reported to the PM. Alas! She could not find time to watch it.

I fondly recall the intensity of his personality and his infectious vivaciousness that was life-affirming. He has now joined the immortals of the film world. I prefer remembering to mourning. His memory will be cherished by millions.